UNLOCK THE COMMUNICATION CODES

Powerful Tools to Radically Improve Your Relationships

Donza Doss

Soul Touch
Publishing

Maui, Hawaii

UNLOCK the Communication Codes:

Powerful Tools to Radically Improve Your Relationships

Copyright © 2018 by Donza Doss

Soul Touch
Publishing

Published by Soul Touch Publishing
Maui, Hawaii

First Edition
Printed in the USA

Cover and interior design by Brian Moreland
Edited by Brian Moreland

Image key stock file ID: 167172245 - iStock license
Image keyhole stock file ID: 479484708 - iStock license
Image background stock file ID: 477285929 - iStock license
Image brain head stock file ID: 849696506 - iStock license

ISBN: 978-0-692-07688-0

I dedicate this book to my family.
If it wasn't for you I would not have gone down this
powerful spiritual path of self discovery.
Thank you!

Acknowledgments

I would like to acknowledge all of my new beautiful Hawaiian friends who have become like my family in such a short time. For showing me so much love, support, and aloha as I embark upon this wonderful journey of writing and living my dream on Maui.

I wish to thank Lisa Klein, for being such a great sister. Her loving and compassionate heart has blessed my life in so many ways. She listened as I read my book to her and was very excited for me. I love you always!

Many thanks also go out to my dear friends: Larissa Joy Roberts, for being such an incredible friend! She has shared her brilliant, creative, talented, sweet heart with me unconditionally. She encouraged, listened, and has been someone I can count on this past year. Sarah Faith Bernstein, for being such a true and loyal friend. She has such integrity and a heart of gold! She was willing to help in any way she could as I finished this book. She read and listened to many of the chapters when I first started writing. Christina Litman, for being my soul sister! Her compassionate heart has touched my soul. If it wasn't for Christina and her family I probably wouldn't be living on Maui. For listening to my book as I read many chapters to her. She was excited and encouraged me to do my best.

Lilia Biniaris, for being one of my best friends here! She has the kindest, biggest, most beautiful heart. She has been such a bright light in my world. For that I am eternally grateful. Janet Baldwin, for being such a great friend and support. Her kind, thoughtful, and loving nature has really touched my heart. Mayza Clark, for always being there when I needed love and nurturing. She is so generous, loving, and such an angel. I am grateful everyday to God that we met. Diane Ferguson, for your constant love and support in my life. For being an incredible listener and beautiful friend. Kellee Lofftus, for being my best friend from childhood, loving me unconditionally through everything. She is brilliant, beautiful, and will always hold a special place in my heart. Deanna Sweet, for her constant love and support. She is so generous, thoughtful and a one of a kind friend. LaDonna Kumar, for coming back into my life this past year and sharing many of her beautiful gifts. For listening to my book and for her deep, positive, insights and support. Thank you. I am eternally grateful.

Beth Klerekoper, for being my go-to girl. Her compassion and empathy has profoundly touched my heart. She is such an incredible listener and supports me emotionally like no other. For that I'm forever grateful! Jonathan Biondolillo, for being a great friend! His kind and thoughtful ways make me smile. Sophia la Fleur, for listening to my book and giving spiritual love and support. Michael Thomson, for listening to my book and for all of your support. To my niece, Jenny Johnson, for her love and support and for listening as I read to her. Thanks to Maire Holmes, for her brilliant, creative support in my life. A special thank you to my brilliant editor, designer, writer, and most of all my wonderful friend, Brian Moreland. Without his hard work and dedication this book would have never been possible. I am forever grateful!

Thank you to everyone who listened, supported, and gave encouragement along the way. Blessings and love to you all.

Table of Contents

Introduction

Are you ready to improve your relationships? Are you ready to learn several new, powerful ways that you can begin communicating with others? I've been wanting to write a book on communication for years now. I'm living in Maui, Hawaii, listening to my spirit and following my dreams. I have the time to sit, focus, and write many things I've learned over the past 25 years when it comes to relationships and communication.

What I've really noticed is the lack of communication that's been happening between most of us. Since social media has swept the planet, it seems that the quality, intimacy, and depth of connection have been lost. I wrote this book in order to share my knowledge, skills, and personal insights, in a practical way, to help make it easier for you and everyone who reads this book to communicate more effectively.

How will I do this, you may be wondering? Through simple, yet powerful and radical, techniques I call Communication Codes. These will give you the tools needed to assist you as we unlock these codes of communication and reveal the many basic breakdowns that occur in language and communication.

After going on my own transformative journey, I have been a life coach, NLP Master Trainer, and Certified Master Hypnotherapist for over 25 years. Working with many couples has shown me that people need the tools in this book to have more harmonious, fulfilling relationships. Whether you're goal is to improve friendships, your marriage, romantic or business relationships, these tools can help you bridge the communication gap that so easily happens between people. I have found the one ingredient that will help save your relationships or marriage and put you back on the road to intimacy and connecting once again. I will point out the things we do, often unconsciously, that sabotage us and keeps us from connecting deeper and getting what we want.

As you read this book, you will learn many insights about which channels of communication you are doing that are working and which channels that aren't. How to find out what channel you and your partner have been coming from, how to get you both on the same channel to create a stronger foundation and intimacy.

You will learn the importance of rapport, what it is and why it is essential in any relationship. What to do when we break rapport and how to reestablish it once it is broken. You will also discover the most effective ways to speak to people, set boundaries, gain power over your emotional triggers, become a better listener, and so much more. This book will give many examples and practical tools for you to utilize and help navigate your way to the relationship of your dreams.

Communication Code 1

Speak the Same Channels

When it comes to communication it seems that we could all use a few more tools under our belts. The one complaint I hear the most from many couples I coach is that he or she just doesn't listen. Or that they both may listen but do not hear what each other is saying. Both parties are correct because without some basic information on how communication works, you will definitely find yourself feeling frustrated and completely unheard.

We all communicate on different channels. Some people think in pictures, which is called the *visual* channel. Some people think in words, which is called the *auditory* channel. Others think in feelings, which is called *kinesthetic*.

There are no right or wrong channels. For some of you this may be new information. I will be teaching some basic NLP technology, which stands for Neuro-

Linguistic Programming. In short, NLP is a learning system based on how language programs our brain, in particular the subconscious or unconscious mind, and teaches many advanced skills for self-improvement and communicating with self and others. While I'm combining many different teachings in one book, I do share some highly effective NLP techniques that I've been using in my coaching practice for years.

One thing I've learned is that the words we use have an effect on other people's minds. For instance, if I say, "DON'T think of a purple pig," what did you just do? Thought of a purple pig, I bet. Our unconscious mind drops out negative words, like "don't" and "not." For example, if you tell a child, "DON'T slam the door," they'll see a picture of the door slamming. The unconscious mind hears the command "Slam the door," and the result often is the child slams the door. A better way to say it would be "Close the door softly." Using advanced communication skills, we learn to say things in a more positive way.

Now, how do you know what channel you and your partner are?

The Eyes Reveal the Channels

It has been said that the eyes are the windows to the soul. They also reveal how a person thinks, whether in pictures, words, or feelings. You can determine people's primary channels by watching where their eyes move when they speak. *Visual* people will continually look up, often to the left or right. That's because they are thinking in pictures and seeing what they are thinking about. *Auditory* people will move their eyes from ear to ear, because they are thinking in sounds and words. *Kinesthetic* people will look down toward the floor and to *their* right side. They are accessing how they feel about what you both are talking about. The fourth primary channel is *Auditory Digital (AD)*. These people hear their voice talking inside their head and think very technical, like processes and systems. *Auditory Digital* people are often engineers, computer programmers, and people who work with technology. To practice reading people's eyes, watch children talking, public speakers giving a speech, and people you're having a conversation with. As they talk, they will constantly look in the direction that they are thinking. Below is a chart that illustrates the eye patterns.

**Eye Patterns to Determine
People's Primary Channels**

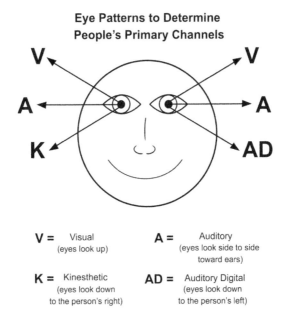

V = Visual (eyes look up)		**A =** Auditory (eyes look side to side toward ears)
K = Kinesthetic (eyes look down to the person's right)		**AD =** Auditory Digital (eyes look down to the person's left)

Calibration

What are some other ways to know what channel you and your partner are?

You begin to recognize a person's state of mind by observing and reading nonverbal signals like the different distinctions in body language, facial expression, skin tone, and color changes, like blushing, how often they touch you, and how fast or slow they talk. Reading these subtle signals is called *calibration* in NLP. Learning calibration is a powerful skill that will help you discover your channel and other people's channels quicker. Calibration is another word for measuring. It is simply noticing what's going on in other people. When people talk fast and look up a lot, they are usually visual. When people talk more monotone and shift their eyes from side to side, toward their ears, they are auditory. When people talk slower and look down to the right, they are more kinesthetic. Kinesthetic people are touchy-feely, so if they are touching your arm, putting their hand on your shoulder, or talking really close, they're usually kinesthetic.

Knowing people's channels is key to effectively communicating with others. Otherwise, we're talking on different channels and experiencing communication breakdowns. Here's a great example: my father was auditory, my mother was kinesthetic, and I am very visual. I talk fast, think fast, and see pictures in my mind. It was extremely difficult to have a conversation with my father, because he would say things like "Listen to me. We need to talk." He would say it in this monotone voice that I couldn't hear or listen to without causing stress and anxiety in my entire body.

Speaking from my visual channel, I would say, "*Look*, don't you *see* it's clear as day?"

He would say, "*Listen*, can you *hear* me?"

As I spoke fast using visual words and he spoke medium speed and monotone using auditory words, he didn't *see* what I was saying and I couldn't *hear* what he was trying to tell me. My kinesthetic mother, speaking with a slow southern drawl, would say things like, "It just doesn't *feel* right." This would confuse me and surely my father, because I was trying to see what Mom was feeling, and Dad was trying to hear it.

If I had not learned about the different channels, then my parents and I would have never been able to communicate with each other. There would always have been this disconnect between us. When I learned these distinctions and began to speak in my father's auditory channel, he lit up like a candle! It was so amazing and exciting to see the reaction and connection we created when I spoke in his channel. The same thing happened with my mother, as well, as I slowed down my speech and spoke to her in her kinesthetic channel. When I talked with my mother, she told me how my dad was so impressed how he could talk to me and I could finally listen and hear him. He sang my praises and said he couldn't believe how much I had matured. The only thing I did differently was I changed my language and shifted out of visual and into auditory and kinesthetic channels. I slowed my pace down and started speaking in Mom's and Dad's tempos. It was truly incredible to "see, hear, and feel" the difference in our communication. Not only did I get more on their level, I also opened up my own auditory and kinesthetic channels. When you develop your non-primary channels, you develop your mind's ability to think in pictures, words, and feelings.

— IF YOU WANT TO BE HEARD AND LISTENED TO IN THE MOST EFFECTIVE WAY, THEN FIND OUT WHAT CHANNEL YOU AND YOUR PARTNER ARE COMMUNICATING FROM. —

To make it easier, you must first identify your own channel. Which feels more comfortable for you? Do you speak fast, more monotone, or do you talk slowly? Remember there are no right or wrong channels. Practice opening up each of your channels by listening to the tone, pace, pitch, and volume of the person with whom you are speaking to. Notice how fast or slow they are talking, then match their speed. When you shift to the other person's channel, you will be amazed how easy it is to get into rapport and communicate with them. You only have to stay in their channel for 10 to 15 minutes to create the connection. By doing that you will notice right away how everything just flows. Then when you shift to your natural channel, they will usually follow.

For instance, if you are visual and your partner is

kinesthetic, then slow your speaking down and drop into your partner's slower channel for those 10 to 15 minutes. Then, as you begin to pick up the pace back to your channel, your partner will begin to talk faster and speak more in your visual channel. One thing to note is that if you start talking too fast with a kinesthetic person, they will not be able to hear you as well. Also, it's very uncomfortable for them and they usually want to end the conversation quickly. So ramp up the speed gradually, from talking slow, to medium tempo, to how you normally speak. The reverse would be for a kinesthetic person who wants to match a visual person. You would talk fast like them for 10 to 15 minutes, gain rapport, then gradually ramp down the speed of your talking to your comfortable tempo. Auditory people speak in a middle tempo, so you only have to adjust the speed of your talking a little, faster or slower, when speaking with a visual or kinesthetic person.

We all want our communication to flow effortlessly, especially with our partners. When you both are aware of each other's channels, then it gets even easier the more you practice being in *their* dominant channel. Rapport and connection gets easier too. You will both feel like you are more alike, because through matching each other's channels, you are literally syncing up your brains on the same wavelength. Calibrating and then matching channels is how you bridge the gap between you and someone who thinks and talks very different than you. This is even more powerful when both people in the relationship know how to adjust their channels and consciously make an effort to match their partner's primary channel.

Speak Their Words

The goal is to learn to open all of your channels so you can be comfortable talking with anyone and everyone. One way to be aware of people's channels is to listen to the words they use and then speak those words back to them. Visual people speak in visual words, like "look, see"; Auditory people speak with words that relate to the ears, like "hear, listen"; and Kinesthetic people say words that relate to the body, like "feel, touch." Here are some sensory-based words that will help you identify other people's channels and your own.

VISUAL	AUDITORY	KINESTHETIC	AUDITORY DIGITAL
See	Hear	Feel	Think
Aim	Tell	Touch	Understand
Bright	Talk	Handle	Compute
Vision	Listen	Fall	Comprehend
Picture	Sing	Push	Thought
Look	Noise	Grasp	Analyze
Clear	Tone	Tackle	Figure
Image	Whisper	Throw	Manage
Scan	Loud	Massage	Effective
Reflect	Shout	Support	Logic
Glow	Silent	Balance	Useful
Watch	Argue	Smooth	Efficient
Dark	Yell	Catch	Relevant
Glare	Praise	Unite	Objective
Sight	Quiet	Grasp	Ideal
Appear	Music	Rough	Example
Show	Squeal	Hurt	Consider
Dim	Ring	Cut	Competent
Visible	Describe	Probe	Apply
Reveal	Voice	Soft	Rational

You will also see another auditory channel called Auditory Digital (AD). These people are more left-brain, analytical, logical, linear type thinkers. It is very useful to know when someone is communicating on that channel. Once you practice learning the different words from each channel, you can right away start creating a deeper rapport and connection with that person.

Communication Code 2

BUILD RAPPORT

One of the key secrets to connecting with people on a deep level is through building rapport.

What is rapport?

Merriam-Webster's Dictionary defines rapport as "a friendly, harmonious relationship; especially : a re-lationship characterized by agreement, mutual un-derstanding, or empathy that makes communication possible or easy." (www.merriam-webster.com)

Rapport is the ability to relate to others in a way that creates trust, understanding, and connection. It is the ability to see another person's point of view and get them to understand yours. You don't have to agree with their point of view or even like it. You just need to understand where they're coming from. Sharing rapport makes any form of communication easier. People like people who are like themselves. When we find things in common with each other, it builds rapport faster and trust begins to be established. Successful interactions, whether with your partner, family, friends, or professional relationships, depend largely on our ability to establish and maintain rapport.

Importance in Similarities

There are two ways to see other people. You can choose to pay attention to the differences or the similarities between you. When you focus on the things that are similar, you create a deeper rapport more quickly. When things feel more familiar you usually feel more comfortable and safe. You can always find things you have in common with someone, even if it is just being human. Likewise, there will always be differences between you and another.

If you focus primarily on the differences, you will find it harder to establish rapport. By paying more attention to what you both have in common, resistance will usually disappear and cooperation will improve. With practice it becomes easy to find what we share with other people and focus on those commonalities. Here are a few techniques to help build rapport with anyone.

1. Pacing

Rapport is established and maintained by pacing and matching. By definition, this is the process of moving as the other person moves and speaking at the speed another person speaks—fast, medium, slow. Pacing or matching accepts the other person's behavior and meets them in their model of the world. It is about reducing the differences between yourself and others at an unconscious level.

You can pace or match many different aspects of behavior. Pacing is mostly used in the words and voice tempo, speed, and will build a deeper quality of rapport when you can pace people. Of course, if the other person is aware you are matching their behavior it becomes mimicking. Obvious attempts to blatantly "copy" people or "mime" their movements will break rapport. Successful pacing is done subtly and appears to the other person at an unconscious level. Often times, you will naturally match and pace people without even thinking about it. To see pacing in action, watch kids or teenagers who are friends talking to one another. When one hyper kid talks excitedly, his or her friend will talk excitedly too. Same goes if one kid is talking slow, say because they are tired or feeling down about something, their friend will talk slow with them. It's human nature to pace or match someone we feel a connection with.

When rapport is established, you can influence the other person's behavior. If you would like to know if you have rapport, make a movement and notice if they follow you. For instance, you might scratch your head and see if the other person does the same. Next time you're sitting across the table from someone, casually lean forward or back, then notice how long it takes them to mirror how you're sitting. When you have a deep enough rapport, then you can begin to lead and direct the person in a way that is comfortable for you. In other words, if I am visual and my sister is auditory, if I speak in the auditory channel long enough to establish rapport with her, then I will be able to go to my visual channel and she will follow and go to my visual channel as well.

2. Matching and Mirroring

Matching and mirroring are behaviors we all do naturally. What happens when someone talks to a small child? They might kneel down to the child's height, talk more slowly (or excitedly). Romantic couples in restaurants often seem to be engaged in a dance, leaning and smiling in mirrored postures. This just happens effortlessly when we are in deep rapport. You can also match consciously when you want to create rapport, say during a job interview or on a first date with someone. Watch their body posture, and then subtly match and mirror them. If they sit back with their leg crossed, wait 10 to 15 seconds, then sit back and cross your leg. If they sit forward, wait a minute, then you sit forward. As long as you're casual about it, your matching will go unnoticed. Have you ever noticed how awkward it feels to be sitting and someone talks to you but remains standing? It feels awkward, right? That's because you are physically out of rapport. You'll feel the urge to ask them to take a seat with you or you may wish them to go away. Or you may stand up to talk to them so that awkward feeling goes away. I must emphasize that matching someone is a very effective way to maintain rapport.

3. Breathing

Breathing is the deepest and fastest way to create rapport. You match the rate of a person's breathing, where they are breathing (chest, abdomen, or stomach) or how deep, shallow, fast or slow. When you begin to match their breathing for only a few minutes, you will notice how close and connected you feel. It is important to note that if someone is having breathing issues, or in a state of anxiety, you may begin to pick up on what they are feeling and experience those same feelings when you're doing this technique. So make sure to stop if you if you feel any kind of discomfort at all.

4. Voice

Matching the pace, volume, pitch, tone, and type of words is a little tricky to learn but worth it. You never have to match all these aspects. Choose one. If a person is talking slowly, slow down. If they speak softly, drop your volume. If they speed up, allow yourself to do the same. Learning to calibrate the subtle distinctions in the voice will help you identify where to match them and create rapport more quickly. This is very powerful in experiencing deep intimacy with your partner. Picture yourself and your partner enjoying a romantic dinner, both speaking softly to one another. By naturally matching your voices, you stay in deep rapport. If you choose to lead your partner from one state to another, say from overexcited to calm, then first match where they are at, noticing their tone, pace or volume, then gradually change your own. Once you are in rapport, they should follow your lead. If you find yourself breaking rapport, then return to matching them, before attempting to lead again.

Calibrating voice is also very useful in sales. When you speak with customers and clients using their tone, volume, or tempo, you can create a strong connection with them and win over their trust. This works extremely well over the phone.

5. Beliefs and Values

When you genuinely make an effort to understand another person's beliefs and values without judgment, that can also create very deep rapport. Once again, you do not have to agree with them or change any of your own values; the goal is to understand.

6. Language Patterns

Matching language patterns is a very effective rapport technique. When you use the same sensory-based words to describe things and processes, the person feels understood.

Listen for their *power* words. Power words are the words that are impacting the person's emotional state. So you want to listen to their words that may trigger the impact on what they are feeling. We've often learned to paraphrase what someone says rather than use the same words. It's called active listening. This is a mistake when it comes to rapport. We attach particular words to corresponding experiences. If someone says she "wants to be needed" and you talk about her "usefulness," you can definitely break rapport. It would be better to say to her, "You are *needed*," using the word she just gave you. Throughout your conversations, make sure you continue to repeat back the same words people use so you keep in rapport. It's even more effective when you use the sensory-based words people are using. Also knowing what channel they are in so you can utilize those words in their channel will create and maintain rapport.

Another example, when I was selling my home in Dallas my first realtor didn't know anything about rapport. Whenever I would say how excited I was to be selling my home and moving to Maui, he would come back and say, "Don't get too worked up because it's going to take a lot of time to sell it." I fired him and found the perfect realtor, RoseMarie LaCoursiere, who would say things like "I know you're so excited and I'm excited for you." She sold my house in one hour for full asking price. She had great rapport skills and really listened to my needs.

Your Super Powerful, Secret Skill: Combining Rapport Techniques

When you combine two or more of the six techniques I just shared, you increase the level of rapport you can have with someone exponentially. This is the difference between feeling like you are acquaintances and feeling like you are close friends, best buds, or even soul mates, soul brothers, or soul sisters.

After learning someone's primary channel, combine these rapport techniques:

- match and pace the speed, pitch, tone of their voice
- match their body posture
- speak their sensory-based words
- speak their power words
- match their breathing (if they take a long, deep breath, do the same)
- be understanding of their beliefs and values

An example would be an auditory or visual person slowing down their talking to match a kinesthetic person, while at the same time using sensory-based words like "feel" and "touch" and physically touching their arm or shoulder (*after* they've touched you first). As I said before, most kinesthetic people are touchy-feely, they need physical touch to feel connected. But let them lead the touching so you know they are comfortable with it. Using kinesthetic words at a slow speed, and breathing slow and deep, will make the kinesthetic person feel deeply connected to an auditory or visual person.

Combining sensory-based words and matching voice and body language will work for connecting with any person—just figure out their primary channel and adjust to their tempo, words, and body posture. This is so powerful that two total strangers who just met can feel like they've known each other for years. Just imagine what this will do for your relationship if you are a couple seeking to create a deeper connection or reconnect after months or years of feeling disconnected.

Learning these basic rapport-building techniques will enhance the quality of your communication and your relationships. Practicing them every day as you talk to people makes life so much easier, because you see, hear, feel, and understand the importance of creating rapport. You will also notice less arguing and fighting in your relationship, and you will be in agreement more often. Especially when you are speaking each other's language and being on the same channel (visual, auditory, kinesthetic).

— RAPPORT IS THE FOUNDATION FOR GOOD COMMUNICATION. —

Another thing to be aware of is how we have a basic assumption that everyone thinks and feels the same way as we do. It was a huge wakeup call when I learned that everyone doesn't think in pictures the same way I do. It truly changed my interactions when I understood that people think differently than I do. Some filter the world through sounds and voices while others think in feelings and touch. Some people can't even visualize pictures at all. Before you assume that your friends or family think the same way as you, begin to ask questions and watch the direction their eyes go. Identify their primary channels then focus on building rapport with people when having a conversation or starting a relationship. After that, communication gets easier.

Communication Code 3

FILTERING AND SORTING

Another important thing to know in communication is how people filter and sort information and where they place their attention, either primarily on themselves or the needs of others. The Attention Direction Filter is about the investment of our attention with respect to self or others. Do you mostly put your attention on the needs of others, or on yourself? When you have a filter, information can't get through in the same way. A coffee filter makes sure that the grounds can't get through and only allows the water to pass. In relationships it's helpful to know what filter you and your partner are coming from.

Sorting Self-to-Self

People who sort self-to-self are focused on their own thoughts, feelings, beliefs, preferences, ideas, wants, and needs. When my attention direction is on self,

I am evaluating information based on how it affects me. I then make decisions about what is good for me personally in the long and/or short term.

An example of sorting self-to-self is when I worked with a married couple. The woman came into the relationship without being able to contribute financially as much as he could. The man was very wealthy and in love. They were building a new house together and the woman didn't like many of the ideas that her husband was doing to the home. He did whatever he wanted because it was his money, and his wife felt as though she had to go along with everything and have it his way, because he was paying for everything. The man kept completely sorting self-to-self and didn't bother to even ask his new wife what she thought about how he designed, decorated, or even where he was putting the pool. She kept saying how she didn't come into the relationship with any money. So in her mind she had no say at all. He would have kept doing this behavior of sorting self-to-self if they hadn't come for a session. After teaching them about the two different filters, the man realized that he was sorting only for his wants, needs, and desires and not considering his wife's wants, needs, and desires. He thought that she liked everything or she would have said something. He actually didn't mind at all having her input. There was simply a disconnect in their communication. We had an excellent session with a breakthrough for both of them, because the woman would have been resentful and would have withheld how she was feeling, and this could have ultimately ended badly for this couple.

Sorting Self-to-Others

When I am sorting to others, I am attending to what others value, believe, think, feel, need, and want. This ability is essential to working and getting along with others, particularly in any kind of leadership, coaching, or counseling role.

Nurturing, valuing, and developing others, whether it be children, customers, or employees, is a long-term relationship development strategy, as well as a way to feel good. One of the powerful ways to overcome depression is to stop focusing on your own self and help other people who are worse off. When you help others, your heart becomes filled with gratifying feelings which can really lift your spirits. Examples of when people sort self-to-others include a mother who does things for her children, a father who works to provide for his family, people who volunteer for charities or do missionary work in other countries. Some careers like being a doctor, nurse, fireman, first responder, or a minister, priest, or nun are primarily sorting self-to-others. Mother Teresa devoted her whole life to the needs of others.

Considering the consequences of your actions and decisions on other people enables consultation and participation. Noticing the effects of your communication enables rapport. So think about whether you primarily sort-to-self or sort-to-others.

We all filter in both ways at different times. There is no right or wrong, just know that when we sort self-to-self on a continual basis it can come across as overly selfish or self-centered and break rapport quickly. The reason is that the other person doesn't get any air time (communication) for themselves, because you may be focusing too much on yourself. Also, when people sort self-to-self they usually don't acknowledge or validate what you say. For example, I met a new friend and she kept talking about herself for over an hour without asking any questions about my life at all. When I finally did say something casual like "Look, I just bought these new shoes," she didn't even respond in any way. She immediately said, "I just bought a new pair of shoes too." Which is great that she did, but I felt out of rapport because she was constantly keeping the conversation about *her*. It's okay to talk about yourself and your needs, just make sure you acknowledge what the other person says first before you go back to sorting self-to-self again.

Remember, we all need to feel validated and heard. I did finally share with my friend about these different distinctions and she realized how often she sorts self-to-self. I use to sort self-to-self a lot of the time, as well, without being aware I was doing it. I love to talk and I love to listen to others as well. Learning how to balance this aspect between yourself and others will make a powerful impact on your ability to maintain rapport and improve the quality of your communication and relationships.

In addition, it is important to notice the body language and voice tones of others. If you continue sorting to yourself more often, then you won't notice if someone is angry, bored, or just not interested. On the flip side, if you primarily sort self-to-others, always putting others' needs before your own, you can put stress on yourself, your body, and your partners. An example would be a mother who sacrifices all her needs, wants, and desires for her family. Or someone who devotes all their time and energy to work or a cause and not enough to their spouse, children, and home. It's best to find a balance when it comes to filtering, sorting, and relating to each other. Paying attention to the way you filter information and sort what's important can create an awareness that helps you maintain harmony and rapport.

Communication Code 4

AVOID WITHHOLDING

What is withholding?

Whenever you do not share your feelings, thoughts, needs, or desires to your partner, that is withholding. A lot of times I hear couples say that they withheld because they were afraid of their partner's reaction. What I say to them and have them repeat after me is "IF I DON'T SHARE IT, I WEAR IT." Because this is so important, it's worth repeating here:

— IF YOU DON'T SHARE IT, YOU WEAR IT. —

What does that mean exactly? If you keep things hidden because of fear, or if you're walking on eggshells with your partner, then chances are there are deeper issues and more work to be done between you. Also, it can affect your health in a very negative way if you keep withholding your true feelings inside.

In addition to being a life coach, I was also a sports massage therapist and had many clients that had major health issues. As I got to know some of them, I found out how they had been withholding for years in their relationships, withholding from their bosses, parents, friends, family, and sometimes even with themselves. It was truly amazing seeing their body relax and let go whenever they began to share their true feelings. Sometimes the pain would even disappear out of their body after we uncovered what they were withholding. What I have witnessed over the years with couples is that when they have the courage to stop withholding, there is a depth and level of intimacy that occurs for them.

You must remember to create rapport before you start to open up with your partner about negative thoughts and feelings. If rapport isn't established first, then you are more likely going to have an adverse reaction from your partner. One of the most effective ways to start opening up is to ask your partner if they could take a few minutes to talk. Then say, "I have something I want to share with you, and I'm afraid you may have a reaction or be upset with what I'm going to tell you."

If it's something you know they will probably get upset with then it prepares your partner before you even say anything. In other words, it buffers the impact to your partner and allows you to communicate more freely. If it's something that's not going to have a negative reaction, then you may want to ask yourself,

What is the real reason I'm withholding? Sometimes it's because we may not want to get into a deep discussion because we fear it will be too time consuming. Or that it may open a Pandora's box and you're just not sure how to work it out. Whatever the case, it is important to know that withholding doesn't make for a deep, intimate relationship with your partner.

I used to be the biggest withholder ever! What I learned as a child was that if I told the truth of what I was thinking and feeling I would still get in trouble. So at a very young age I started withholding what I was thinking, feeling, believing, or needing. It seemed to be easier because I didn't want to rock the boat in any way or get in trouble. Times are much different these days. We allow children to speak instead of saying, "Children are to be seen and not heard." Remember those days? Have the courage to speak up. We are no longer children and our partners are not our parents. Although we act as though they are sometimes, don't we? We have the right to speak up and tell our truths. Now we get to choose how we do it. Are we going to be clean or are we going to be mean when we share and communicate?

Communication Code 5

SPEAKING CLEAN VS. MEAN

When it comes to communications with our partners, family, children, friends, and co-workers, it's obvious that we speak differently to each other. Have you ever noticed that the way you speak to your family is totally different than the way you speak to your friends?

When we feel closer to our family and in our relationships, it seems that we think that it gives us permission to say whatever we want to say to them and in any way that we please. Sometimes those ways can be harsh, unkind, and just plain mean.

My hopes for writing this chapter is for everyone to become more aware of his or her words, tones, and intentions. You've heard many times growing up that "if you don't have something nice to say to someone, then don't say anything at all." What I'm saying is ... once you stop the withholding and start becoming more honest in what you're feeling, then it is less likely that you will want to say something mean to those around you. Especially the people you love the most.

— INSTEAD OF BEING MEAN, BE CLEAN IN YOUR LANGUAGE. —

When I say be "clean in your language," I'm not talking about swearing or cursing. I'm talking about being clear, direct, honest, and kind in your conversations. You never have to be mean or sarcastic. Research has found that when people are being sarcastic that they are usually covering up anger and resentment of some kind. Those words meant to be funny can actually be malicious jabs at another person. I think we know the difference when we are being sarcastic or when we are just joking. If your sarcastic words have any intent to hurt someone, put them down, or harm another in anyway, then you know that you're coming from a mean place.

How do you stop this mean behavior?

First, you must be aware that you are doing it. If you are being critical, judgmental, or sarcastic you must stop. If that means walking away for a moment so you can regroup, then do that. Secondly, you can make an agreement with your family and partner that if you snap off in any way that sounds harsh, abusive, or unkind, then they have the right to tell you to stop it! Sometimes you may not even realize how sharply or harshly you are speaking to someone. If your primary communication channels are visual or kinesthetic, then you need to pay attention to how you speak to people, especially if anyone close to you is auditory. Auditory people are much more sensitive to sounds, tones, and words. The impact on auditory people can be much worse, because they listen more and your words are very powerful and can affect them deeply. It's not only the auditory channels that are affected; the visual and kinesthetic channels are as well. Start today by noticing how you're speaking to those around you. Are you being clean or are you being mean? Consciously begin to speak in a softer, kinder tone with nicer words, and you will be amazed at the positive impact your words have on the people around you.

I used to not even hear my tone when I spoke to people. It sometimes came across in a sharp and harsh way. I didn't have a clue how my words landed with people. I truly didn't hear my tone or words, and I had to clean up so many of my past relationships and issues with my family. When I started to become aware of and understand the impact that my harsh tone and negative words were having on people it changed my life.

What I learned most is that I was being just as harsh and mean to myself. The negative ways I would speak to myself was very unkind, and that was painful to see. When I started being clean in my expression to others, I noticed right away how I stopped being so mean to myself. It was such an empowering moment and I've had many breakthroughs when it comes to my communication with myself and others. I became full of gratitude and appreciation, because I was really happy to have broken the unhealthy, yet familiar, pattern that had been running my life for years.

How do you speak to yourself when you make a mistake or do something you know isn't good for you? Do you beat yourself up and punish yourself for days? If so, remember to stop in mid-thought and step away. Moving your body physically will help you stop being so mean to yourself. Also ask for feedback with the people in your life to remind you if you're being unkind to yourself or to them. Once you become accountable for what you're doing, it gets easier to stop the behavior.

— OWN YOUR MEAN BEHAVIOR, THEN YOU CAN STOP IT. —

Be gentle with yourself and the person who may need feedback or support. Remember, what you put out you will definitely get back. If you're going around speaking harshly and being mean to people, you will find yourself living in a world where everyone is talking harshly back to you. So become more conscious now of how your words impact those around you and yourself.

What if members of your family and partner aren't willing to speak cleanly and kindly to you? What if you don't feel safe enough with the person, then what do you do?

I grew up with a father that, if you didn't listen to

him, he would raise his voice and keep yelling until you did listen. I was afraid so much of the time of his reaction. Only after I learned about rapport, did things change. Rapport is so effective at making communication easier. You can say most anything to anyone if you have created enough rapport with them. I want people to stop being afraid to communicate authentically with one another. Improving your rapport skills is essential if you're wanting to build a deeper, intimate connection with your partner and family. So when you have an issue with someone, get rapport first, then be authentic in what you share, and always remember to be kind as you talk to them.

When I started speaking clean and being nicer to the people around me, they changed as well. You never have to be mean, even if you're not feeling safe. Remember how you would want to be spoken to and practice working on your rapport skills. It's up to you to set boundaries with those around you and for yourself.

Communication Code 6

SETTING BOUNDARIES

What are boundaries?

Wikipedia defines *personal boundaries* as "guidelines, rules, or limits that a person creates to identify reasonable, safe, and permissible ways for other people to behave towards them, and how they will respond when someone passes those limits."

Types

Here are four boundary types, proposed by Nina Brown, author of *Children of the Self-Absorbed* and other books:

Soft – A person with soft boundaries merges with other people's boundaries. Someone with a soft boundary is easily a victim of psychological manipulation.

Spongy – A person with spongy boundaries is like a combination of having soft and rigid boundaries. They permit less emotional contagion than soft boundaries but more than those with rigid. People with spongy boundaries are unsure of what to let in and what to keep out.

Rigid – A person with rigid boundaries is closed or walled off so nobody can get close either physically or emotionally. This is often the case if someone has been the victim of physical, emotional, psychological, or sexual abuse. Rigid boundaries can be selective, which depend on time, place or circumstances and are usually based on a bad previous experience in a similar situation.

Flexible – Similar to selective rigid boundaries but the person exercises more control. The person decides what to let in and what to keep out, is resistant to emotional contagion and psychological manipulation, and is difficult to exploit.

In every relationship boundaries are important and need to be established. Learning how to set them and knowing what to do when yours are crossed is crucial in having successful relationships. Set the stage with appropriate boundaries right at the beginning of every relationship. People take their cues for acceptable behavior based on how you speak and act. Seemingly harmless comments can slide quickly into uncomfortable territory. Correct the small infractions immediately so people know where you stand and know that you're willing and able to set boundaries. Some behaviors are never acceptable in a relationship. Verbal and nonverbal behaviors that are never appropriate include: sarcasm, retaliation, intimidation, teasing or taunting, swearing, and inappropriate tones of voice that express impatience or exasperation, screaming or raising your voice. Any kind of physical abuse clearly cannot be tolerated in any relationship. When partners or friends won't honor or respect your boundaries, then it may be time to leave the relationship.

There are "grey areas" around boundaries that require the use of good judgment and careful consideration of the context. For example, when you first meet someone, do you hug them or shake their hand? On the island of Maui in Hawaii most people hug here, so it's not a grey area. In New York, you might get a different reaction if you try to hug someone you just met.

While each separate situation may appear harmless, when put together, they may form a pattern indicating that a boundary has been crossed. It can sometimes be difficult to put your finger on it when a boundary has been crossed. Notice if you're feeling uneasy or uncomfortable. Boundary crossing may begin with seemingly innocent comments or disclosures and escalate from there. Most of the time we let it slide because we may not be fully aware of how we are feeling. Then when you leave the person or situation, you think about how what they did or said made you feel uneasy.

You can still set the boundary even if you think you've missed your chance. It's never too late. If it's someone you want to remain in relationship with, then you must address the boundary issue *immediately*, so the person doesn't forget or so you won't forget. Call them on the phone and be clean and clear in your communication. For instance, you could say, "I noticed when you said that statement I felt uncomfortable. Although I didn't say anything in the moment, I would really appreciate you not speaking that way to me." Or if it's a topic, you can set the boundary and let the person know that you don't talk about politics, religion, or money. Whatever it is that you're not comfortable with.

— SETTING BOUNDARIES IS A HEALTHY WAY TO RESPECT YOURSELF AND COMMUNICATE YOUR COMFORT ZONES TO OTHERS —

What I've learned is that people really appreciate when you set boundaries with them, especially children. It took many years to learn and understand about setting boundaries for myself. In relationships, I was a pleaser and could never say no. People who know me now would never believe that I didn't have good boundaries. But it was very difficult to say "no" and set clear boundaries. I so badly wanted to be loved and I thought if I wasn't a "yes" person then I wouldn't be loved or accepted.

Learning how to set boundaries actually saved my life on many levels and helped with many of my relationships, as well. I learned how to say "no" and feel OK about myself in the process. Setting boundaries meant that I was taking care of my needs and myself.

Setting boundaries for yourself can be difficult at first because you're not used to it. Like anything else, it takes practice and time to get better. This is an important skill to learn, and once you master it, your communication and relationships will improve dramatically.

I had a client who had two children. She couldn't set boundaries with her kids. When she told me how they behaved and how she felt she had no control over them, I thought they had to be teenagers. Turns out, they were nine and eleven-year-old boys and they ran the house. The mother didn't want to argue or fight with them, so she let her sons do anything they wanted. There was no bedtime schedule, no rules or boundaries in place at all. She was a single mom and didn't know what boundaries were herself. The more we uncovered in the session, the more she realized that the reason she wouldn't set boundaries for them was because she felt guilty over the fact that they had no father. He had left and she was the sole provider.

There were many excuses why she let her sons run the house. When finally getting to the truth of her emotions and her guilt, she broke down. It's sometimes easier to bury your head in the sand and not deal with things. That was her reasoning. After teaching her how important boundaries are, especially with children, she began to listen. I coached the boys as well. They were smart kids and knew they ran the house.

We began to put some simple boundaries in place for them. Like having a certain bedtime every night, and having a small amount of time on the computers or games each night. Also helping with the chores. Let me tell you, this was life changing for this mother! At first the children rebelled and didn't like it at all. After a week of the mother staying strong and keeping the boundaries with them in place, these boys were like different kids when I saw them again.

Remember, you get to set the boundaries with your children and for yourself. Once you work through your emotional baggage, then it gets easier to do. Your children will appreciate and respect you more in the long run. Most of all, you will respect yourself.

Communication Code 7

RELEASE EMOTIONAL BAGGAGE

We all have that one box or suitcase that hides in the back of the closet. It's full of many memories that we just can't let go of. This box may contain our childhood treasures like letters from past relationships, or high school yearbooks, trophies from when you were a child, or souvenirs of people we love. No matter how many times we move, we seem to lug that box with us. I have had a hope chest since I was ten years old. My mother used to joke and say, "Honey, I hope someday you get a chest." My hope chest is filled with memories that I've collected most of my life. As long as I keep it tucked away out of sight, then it won't get in the way.

It may be true that a box of your treasures may not be impeding your life. It is possible that it's preventing you from using that extra space in your closet for your benefit. When it came to my hope chest, I thought there were objects from my past that I couldn't live without. I had many feelings and was extremely attached to those objects inside. When I was moving to Maui, I knew I had to let go of some of those *things* that I was still clinging to. What feelings do you hold on to?

Like the memories kept inside my hope chest, we all keep a wellspring of emotions tucked away in our minds. These emotions may be fear, anger, guilt, grief, or sadness. We may pine for the past or fret over the future, when really we could be living in the present. Our minds may feel anxious when we think of letting go of the things that weigh us down emotionally.

Why let go?

Often, we define ourself by the emotions we feel. We say, "I'm angry" or "I'm sad," when in reality we only feel these emotions. By identifying with those feelings we become them. In essence, we become emotional packrats.

When I was younger and just learning about self-improvement, I went to a seminar called "Success without Sabotage" by Patrick Collard. His new ways of teaching, thinking, and learning how to let go of emotional baggage impacted my life deeply. He would have us uncover what our core negative beliefs were about ourselves that he called our *negative birth scripts*. When we uncovered what mine was, I was completely surprised. I had a belief that I wasn't enough. It wasn't conscious at all. I felt as though

I was too much for people most of the time. The process Patrick did to help us find out what our core beliefs were was simple. We each had to think of our most negative thought we had about ourselves and then stand up and just say it. The first thing I said was "I'm not good enough."

He said, "The reason that you're not good enough is because...?" He kept unwinding with each question until you were at the deepest belief. I wasn't sure how to let go at this point because I had never been conscious of that limiting belief before. Once I was aware, then and only then, was I able to let go of the limiting belief. We did many positive exercises that lessened my core belief, and helped me let go of those negative feelings of not being enough. After repeating positive affirmations and encouraging messages, I stopped hiding my feelings. It became easier to let go of those self-defeating thoughts and feelings. You know the ones we say to ourselves that harbor and modify our perception to see only the negative parts of ourselves.

You may tell yourself that playing the victim or hiding from your feelings is easier, and that may be true. Instant gratification feels good, and for a moment the proverbial band-aid conceals the pain. However, leaving the wound untreated can fester and become a much larger problem than when you were first injured. Everything is energy. Our feelings and thoughts send out a vibration, and what you send out to the world is what you receive back. Hanging on to negative emotions takes more energy than it does to just let go. Once you make the choice to let go and start accepting fully where you are emotionally, life gets easier. Release yourself from the negative grip of your own mind. Why let go? Because the freedom feels fantastic!

What's the purpose of holding on?

Security - You may have the need to protect yourself and your loved ones out of fear that they will get hurt or make mistakes. Fears and insecurities can keep us holding on even more than we ever thought possible.

Happy memories - You want to reminisce about your past loves, successes, or when you experienced the feelings of being happy and full of joy.

Self-esteem - You have the need to be the best in every area of your life, so you live in fear of failing or falling short of someone's expectations, which limits your productivity.

Conflicting beliefs - You keep returning to past experiences, going over and over in your mind, either convincing yourself that you were right or feeling guilty for the way you behaved.

Whatever is in your emotional baggage, it is preventing you from living your life now. Having dreams is healthy, but obsessing is crippling. Learning from the past mistakes can be enlightening. But holding on to anger, resentment, or pain can be damaging. Allowing fear and anger to control your behavior restricts other people (partners, friends, children) and may manifest into physical ailments. Chronic negative emotions can cause many health issues.

Clearing Out the Baggage in the Closet

We all have emotional and mental clutter. Some of us may struggle with a particular relationship or temporary emotion, while others may be living with years of self-abuse and emotional hoarding. Whatever the size of your suitcase, it is time to unpack. It may be impossible to get rid of everything (without memories, who are we?), but wallowing in negativity will destroy your chances to feel positive in the present.

Start with acceptance. Identify the emotions you feel and own them. What you can't own will definitely own you. Taking responsibility for your emotions will put you back in the driver's seat, feeling in control of your life once again.

Recognize why you want to keep this emotion around. Like a child clinging tightly to their security blanket when they are scared, holding on to something familiar helps us cope. It's also important to concede that people or events can't make you happy. By holding on to the hope for more money, a better job, that special someone, you are allowing this dearth to dictate your emotions.

Realize what you can't do with these emotions and what you can do instead. Ask yourself what does holding on to these feelings do for you? Do you feel safer? Do you feel happier? Reliving the past or worrying about the future neglects one simple fact: There is nothing you can do about it. Instead, take control of what you can. Be honest with yourself and others.

Unpack your baggage and let it go. This sounds very simple, and it is, but it takes discipline and practice and a willingness to move out of your comfort zone. Be easy on yourself and allow yourself to feel the emotions that come to the surface. If you become present to feeling anger, then feel the anger. If you enter a state of sadness, then fully feel the sadness, allow yourself to cry, until the sorrow passes. And it will. Emotions are like storms: they will come and they will go. The worst thing you can do is be too critical on yourself for feeling whatever you're going through. Also, realize that *now* is the only time you have control of, so it is *now* that you need to respond.

When emotions are connected to a wrong done by someone else, and you feel a charge about that person, forgiveness is the fastest way to let go of past emotional baggage. It doesn't mean you condone anyone's behavior that wasn't appropriate. What it means is that you work on learning the positive lessons from what happened in that experience. When you can begin to forgive then you can start the healing process.

Communication Code 8

LEARN TO FORGIVE

Forgiveness doesn't mean that one has forgotten or excused an offense, simply that one has recognized it and made a conscious decision to let go of the pain it has caused. When forgiving someone, it's not necessary that you also reconcile with the offender.

Some might be inclined to think that reconciliation occurs along with forgiveness, but this is not always the case. You may be able to forgive a family member, for example, who has said or done hurtful things, but it may be harmful, both mentally and physically, to maintain a connection with that family member.

It is possible to forgive someone without minimizing or defending the offense committed. Forgiveness also takes time, even more so if the offense was a serious one. When someone causes significant and traumatic harm, either on purpose or accidentally, true forgiveness can often be challenging. The manner in which a person is able to forgive others depends partially on that person's definition of forgiveness. It is often possible for a person to forgive someone by developing empathy for that person. For others, forgiveness is simply the act of moving past a slight and not holding a grudge; while for others, the process of forgiving someone requires repairing the relationship.

The most important thing I've learned about forgiveness in relationships is that by holding on to the issues, it's only hurting myself and usually my body as well. It will take time and the intention to forgive, and it doesn't mean you have the person back in your life. I used to think if I forgive, then I must have them back in my life. Sometimes you have to just let go if you're dealing with unhealthy, dysfunctional people. You can still love them, but you no longer have to have them in your life.

When it comes to your romantic relationships, you or your partner may need more time to forgive. I recommend seeing a couples therapist, life coach, or even your spiritual adviser to help work through whatever the issues may be. When you can forgive someone there is such an emotional and mental freedom that occurs, and your body feels much lighter and healthier as well. Remember, when you are angry or triggered in any way, it takes longer to let your guard down and open your heart so you can forgive and heal.

Here are a few ways that I learned to forgive. First, write a forgiveness letter. Making sure you know what your intentions are. For example, your intentions in writing this is to release any resentment, anger, or regret. To be free of the hurt and pain so that you can move forward in your life with peace and freedom. You never have to send the letter; it's just for your healing purpose. This technique is profoundly healing. If you're tired of suffering and feeling blocked, I highly recommend this. You can vent and write whatever you feel upset about. You have free reign on what you want to say. Take your time and allow this letter to help with any unresolved feelings or issues that you've been holding onto from the past. It really works and it helped me so much in letting go of negative feelings and forgiving!

Another wonderful process that can be very helpful is called *Ho'oponopono*. It is a Hawaiian word that means "to make right." I learned this back in 1993 and have used it many times. It has allowed me to forgive in ways I never thought possible.

There are four steps:

1. I'm Sorry
2. Please Forgive Me
3. Thank you
4. I Love You

Close your eyes and visualize a stage. Now imagine that you are floating high above the stage, looking down. The person you need to forgive is down below on the stage. Imagine that there is a cord connected to your belly button and that cord is connected to the belly button of the person who is on the stage. Always remember to be disassociated. In other words, you are a good distance above the stage and looking down at the person. Never on the stage with them. Then say these words to the person: "I'm sorry, please forgive me. I love you, and thank you." Then you imagine that the person on the stage says those words back to you. Then you start cutting the cord that connects the two of you. (This cord is called an *aka cord*. There can be one or more aka cords connecting you to the other person). Next, see a big pair of scissors in your mind cutting the cords. This will energetically disconnect you from that person. After you have cut the cords, then see him or her moving off the stage. Watch them float farther and farther away from you, shrinking smaller and smaller in the distance until he or she disappears.

There are many variations of this visualization technique. On YouTube, you can find videos on practicing *Ho'oponopono* and aka cord cutting that you can watch online to help walk you through the process your first time. Choose which method works best for you. It doesn't matter what order you say the four steps. The technique is simple and incredibly effective. The freedom you feel from forgiving someone is amazing! The most powerful feeling is when you can begin to forgive yourself. Now that is life-altering!

Communication Code 9

SHIFT YOUR
EMOTIONAL TRIGGERS

What are emotional triggers?

Have you ever used the phrase that someone "pushes your buttons"? Those "buttons" are emotional triggers. Emotional triggers are usually installed into your mind and nervous system when you experienced something negative or traumatic sometime during your past, like getting scolded by your father or mother. Or maybe a sibling locked you in a closet and you feel claustrophobic in tight places. When put in a position similar to that negative experience, like your boss or partner scolds you with the same tone and intensity that your parent did, strong emotions are stirred up and the reaction can lead to an emotional outburst that you often regret. Or you feel flustered and want to get away from the person or situation immediately. If left unhealed emotional triggers will continue to control you. There are ways you can address these triggers and reduce your negative reaction to them.

Accept Responsibility for Your Reaction

Accept yourself as a powerful person instead of as a victim. Become totally honest with yourself. When you learn to identify what is triggering how you feel in the moment, you give yourself the chance to feel differently, if you want to. You will also have more clarity on what you need to do or what you need to ask for to change your circumstances.

What would your life look like if you were in control of your reactions? How free would you feel if you lived your life by choice? Once you recognize the pattern and can identify the feelings, you can start to become aware of the issue that was triggered. If you look into your past and find the core of that trigger, it will usually stop your reaction or at least calm you down, because you have more understanding and insight as to why it is happening. The faster you notice an emotion is triggered, the sooner you can discover if there is a real threat or not.

I had a breakthrough recently about my judgmental and critical parts of myself. What I discovered was that when I judged or criticized people, it was a way to push them away. It had been a kind of protection to keep myself safe so I wouldn't get hurt, abandoned, or feel the pain of loss in any way. Have you ever noticed that we are more judgmental and critical of the people closest to us? When I realized that I'd been doing this subconsciously, I cried so hard. The greatest gift is that I am now consciously aware and I am willing to look at my issues so they aren't controlling me anymore. It doesn't mean that I won't ever be judgmental or critical again. It means that now I can choose to stop allowing those parts to dictate my life in any negative or unhealthy way. In other words, by owning those sides of myself they aren't owning me like before. It's a power place of healing.

Stop judging or fearing your emotions. If you don't recognize your feelings, you can't change them. It will keep negatively impacting your relationships and prevent you from creating happiness in your life. Once I started recognizing my feelings and became aware of my triggers, it was easier to talk about them and I didn't have to keep judging myself. Be kind and compassionate with yourself and you will notice you are less likely to be triggered. I now welcome my triggers because then I know I still have more to learn about myself.

How to Shift Your Emotional State When Triggered

First, acknowledge to yourself that your emotions have been triggered. In your mind, say something like, "He/She just triggered my feelings." This immediately puts you in power of the emotional state you're presently in and helps you take responsibility for what you're feeling. Your emotional triggers or buttons were already there, someone just pushed them. So, be conscious that you're upset because you've been triggered. Instead of lashing out and blaming the person who triggered you, step away from them, if possible. Then, relax, breathe deep, full cleansing breaths all the way down to your solar plexuses. This will help your body to let go of any tension or tightness very quickly.

Ask yourself, what is this upset reaction trying to do for me that is positive? Most of the time it is distracting you from what you're really feeling, usually anger or fear. Which is covering hurt feelings or some kind of emotional pain. See if you can identify what you're feeling in the moment.

— ONCE YOU IDENTIFY WHAT YOU'RE FEELING, THE UPSET WILL LESSEN IMMEDIATELY. —

Focus on how you would rather feel: peace, calm, relaxed, and centered. Clear your mind and become aware of your body. Also, if you can, get grounded with the earth. Go outside and put your bare feet in the grass. Walk in nature or along a sandy beach and unwind your mind. Doing these simple techniques will start to shift your emotional state as well and get you feeling centered. Your triggers and reactiveness will begin to dissipate. The more you practice your breathing and grounding, the easier it will be to let go of those negative triggers.

Communication Code 10

BE AWARE OF EGO VS. SPIRIT

Are you coming from a place of ego or spirit? I went to a seminar when I was in my twenties, and this man leading it stopped in front of my chair and asked me an unusual question: "Who are you?"

I answered, "I'm Donza Doss."

"Well that's your name, but *who* are you?"

"I am a sports therapist and life coach."

"That's what you do, but who *are* you?" he said.

"Sir, I have no idea what you're talking about."

"Let me ask you something. Do you believe you have a spirit inside of you?"

"Absolutely," I replied.

"You have a mind, body, and ego, but are you those

things?" he asked.

"I have never thought about this in my life," I replied.

"Well, think about it."

"OK, no I'm not those things."

"So, do you believe that your essence is spirit?"

"Yes, I totally do," I said.

He asked, "Did you know that your spirit only knows love, joy, happiness, peace, compassion, kindness, forgiveness, and all the other positive emotions you can feel?"

"No, I've never heard this before," I said.

"Anything that you're feeling other than those positive feelings are part of your ego, and your ego has the consciousness of a seven-year-old. Feelings like fear, anger, guilt, shame, resentment, judgment, making wrong, comparing, blaming, and being critical. Any negative feeling keeps you from remembering that your true essence is spirit. The ego isn't bad or wrong. It keeps you feeling separate and remembering that you are spirit."

I looked down at the floor and shook my head.

"What are you feeling?" he asked.

"I'm in my ego ninety-five percent of the day!"

"I know. We all are."

The seminar leader began to teach us how to become more aware of the ego and what to do when we are in it. Here are the two questions you ask yourself:

Who am I being? When you are upset, or triggered in any way, stop and ask yourself that question: "Who am I being?" When you recognize that you're in your ego, then your ego becomes aware and will usually lessen and let go of the negative emotion and get you back in your spirit. Then you ask the next question.

Who do I want to be? Do you want to be in your spirit or do you want to be in your ego? It's OK if you choose to stay in your ego, as long as you know that you are choosing it and that you will usually stay stuck in that negative emotion. The ego stirs up the emotions and loves to thrive on drama and chaos. Just be aware that those ego feelings can hurt your body and cause more stress in the long run.

I raised my little sister from the time she was thirteen years old until she was eighteen. I began teaching her this distinction of ego vs. spirit soon after she moved in with me. I told her to get my keys and go to the garage and I would be right there. I had a five-speed convertible Mercedes and it was parked in the garage. She decided to start the car not knowing it was in gear, and she had never driven before in her life.

As I'm walking down the hall I hear a huge crash coming from my garage! I ran as fast as I could to the garage, and to my surprise, I saw my car crashed into the wall in front and it went into my dining room. The front end totally smashed! Let me tell you, I had never been so emotionally triggered or in such shock over something before in my entire life! Luckily my sister wasn't injured. Mostly just in shock, as well.

I started yelling, "What were you thinking! What were you doing?"

She was crying and said, "I'm so sorry!" Over and over that's all she kept saying.

I told her to get upstairs and that she was grounded!

As she was walking to the door this little thirteen-year-old girl turned back to me and shouted, "Who are you being right now?!"

I was like "WHAT!"

She shouted it again, "Who are you being right now?!"

I stopped for a moment and yelled back, "I'm being in my ego and I'm going to stay there for a while! Get up in your room!"

My teenage sister using my "stuff" against me. It was brilliant, I must say. Because when she left the garage, I did stop and knew I had to find out why I was so triggered and why I couldn't get out of my ego faster. I stood there and began to question myself. Within minutes, it dawned on me that I was terrified! I had custody of her and was completely responsible for her. The fear kicked in and I started to cry. I knew I had to apologize and clean up the mess made from my emotional trigger and get back in my spirit. I went upstairs and told my sister that she was absolutely right, that I was in my ego and that I was really sorry for yelling at her. She was just trying to be helpful and start the car. I did let her know she was in her ego, as well. She didn't understand when I told her that. "Is it legal for a thirteen-year-old to drive?"

"No," she replied. It was a valuable lesson for both of us.

Do you have the courage to get out of your ego in your relationships? It takes practice and a willingness to do the work and look inside to uncover the truth. Again, it takes being able to recognize that you have been emotionally triggered and take ownership of what you are feeling. Recognizing who you are being in the moment will put you back in alignment with yourself and your spirit. When you begin to listen to your spirit your life will transform. The rewards are worth it.

Communication Code 11

BECOME A BETTER LISTENER

Most people focus more on speaking than on listening. This is an issue that can cause miscommunication and break rapport. When we are speaking we want others to listen. We can get annoyed, offended, or out of rapport if we don't feel heard. Why is it so difficult to pay attention, be present, and listen, especially in our romantic relationships? I believe that social media has caused many people to lose their ability to focus. With so much stimulus coming at us constantly, it does make it much harder to be in the present moment. With cell phones ringing, text messages going off, television blaring, and so many other distractions, it's no wonder that we aren't listening well to one another.

**— TO BECOME EFFECTIVE
IN YOUR COMMUNICATION
YOU MUST LEARN HOW TO LISTEN. —**

Here are a few things that can help you listen better and become more involved with the person you're communicating with now.

First, put your phones on silent when you know you're going to have a longer conversation. You can even put them away if this is going to be a serious one. Most people listen with the intent to react rather than understand. When your partner shares with you something meaningful, listen. I mean really *listen*, being fully present focused intently on what they are saying to you. Do not offer advice, give your opinion, or any kind of feedback unless they ask for it.

Secondly, make eye contact when you're listening. If you want to show that you are really involved in what they're saying, then keep eye contact consistent. No looking out the window or down at the ground or at people passing by. Make the other person the center of your attention and let them know that you're interested and really care about what their talking about.

The third thing and most importantly, stay present in the conversation. Many times our minds bounce around all over the place. If you can clear your mind and stay in the present moment, chances are it will be easier to become more engaged with your partner. The benefits of enhancing your listening skills will pay off in the long run. Often, when we have the opportunity to talk to someone who listens, we find that the best listeners enable us to listen to ourselves.

When listening to people, keep an open mind. Listen without judgment or criticizing what they are saying.

This is imperative if it's your partner and they are talking about their feelings or something important. If you are judging, chances are they won't want to open up and talk to you anymore. That has been such an issue with many couples I have coached. The woman wants the man to open up, and when he does the woman will interrupt, judge, or criticize him. If you're a woman, this will completely shut down your man. It's not only the women who do the judging or criticizing. Men do it as well.

Become responsive when listening to your partner so they know you're listening. Look at them and let them know that you're paying attention to what they're saying. We all crave to be heard.

— RESPONSIVENESS IS A KEY TO LONG LASTING RELATIONSHIPS. —

Your ability to be responsive will determine whether your conversations are enjoyable or if they end in miscommunication. In other words, when your partner shares with you, make a comment back so they know that you've been listening.

I had a couple that came for coaching and the woman was upset. She felt her husband never listened to her, because he didn't respond when she was speaking, nor did he look at her. She felt ignored, unimportant, and insignificant. He finally admitted that he was only half-listening because she talked too fast for him. They were communicating on different channels. Her primary channel was visual and his was auditory digital and kinesthetic. I taught them what I covered in the first Communication Code. In one session the couple learned about each other's channels and how to become more responsive when she was talking. It made such a difference in their marriage. They began to communicate in each other's channels and were finally understanding each other.

Stop Interrupting

This is another big complaint I hear when working with couples. Women tend to interrupt more than men. When we interrupt, it's called a *pattern interrupt*, and it is very difficult to pick up where you left off because your brain often forgets what you were talking about. This seems to happen more frequently with men when it comes to forgetting. It is such a bad habit to interrupt and it is ineffective. Ask yourself what is going on inside of you that has this need to keep interrupting.

— WE ALL MUST WORK TO STOP INTERRUPTING AND LEARN TO BECOME MORE PATIENT WHEN OTHERS ARE TALKING. —

It pains me to admit that I have been a terrible interrupter in the past. I felt I had no control of what blurted out of my mouth sometimes. When I finally uncovered one of the reasons I kept interrupting, I wasn't as surprised as I thought I would be. It was anxiety. I felt if I kept my thoughts inside that I would burst and I just had to interrupt. I did this a lot when I was younger. If anxiety is an issue for you, then you may want to seek professional help. It may be more than just a bad habit that you need to break. Remember, when you interrupt, listening stops. Becoming aware of why you interrupt will ease some of the compulsion and help you become more patient and understanding toward yourself and your partner. Catch yourself. Be aware when you cut someone off. Stop yourself mid-stream and apologize for interrupting. This will take discipline on your part to stop yourself once you've caught yourself in the act. Simply being aware of your interrupting habit and making an effort to change will help you improve your communication immensely. When you are listening to someone and feel the urge to butt in to the conversation, interrupt the interrupter inside your mind, instead of the person who's talking. Stay quiet and keep listening until they've finished or there is a natural break in the conversation.

I had to work really hard to stop interrupting people. I was also afraid I was going to forget what I wanted to say. The real truth is by doing that you are not being totally present with that person, because you are waiting to say what you want instead of listening fully to them. It has taken a lot of constant practice to stop interrupting. When you do stop interrupting, you will notice how you're able to go deeper in the conversation and how your connection grows stronger together. Also, you will appreciate it even more when you're no longer being interrupted or being the interrupter. Remember, we all want to be heard and listened to. Practice every day and become more aware of when you're cutting people off in your conversations.

When you are the one being interrupted, one thing you can do is say to the person, "Can I finish my thought?" I noticed that they will usually apologize immediately and allow you to continue. Also ask yourself what's their intention by interrupting. Most of the time it isn't personal. Once you realize this and understand that they aren't trying to offend you, it will make the behavior more tolerable. It may give you more patience for them if you understand that they're not doing it deliberately to offend you. The more aware you become, the more your relationships will improve, and you will begin to feel much better about yourself and your communication. When your needs are met it creates a deeper intimacy.

What do you do when your partner interrupts on purpose?

I worked with a couple struggling with this very issue. The woman would interrupt her husband constantly on purpose. She felt that she could tell the story more accurately and include more important details than what he would share. The story didn't feel complete to the wife so she would interrupt and add more. If this is your truth, and you are the storyteller being interrupted, then claim your rights and take ownership of the story. Invite the person to share any additional information or details after you have completed the story. So then you won't feel annoyed from being interrupted as much. The wife didn't stop interrupting completely after our session, but her husband started adding more of the details to his stories, which made her feel less irritated. Even though she still chimed in when he was sharing, he said he wasn't as bothered by it since we talked about it.

Communication Code 12

UNDERSTAND YOUR
BASIC HUMAN NEEDS

According to renowned coach and speaker Anthony Robbins, success and happiness can be found by meeting certain needs that are fundamental to human beings. Human beings are motivated by (or can be motivated by) the desire to fulfill six core needs. These needs are not merely wants or desires but profound needs and form the basis of every choice we make.

As we begin to understand what drives our decisions and behaviors on a daily basis, we can develop awareness of the reasons why we do the things we do (like some of the unhelpful strategies we use that impact us physically, mentally, emotionally, socially, and spiritually).

What are the 6 core human needs?

Needs of the Personality

These core human needs are defined by the brilliant Tony Robbins, who combined his studies of NLP with Maslow's Hierarchy of Needs.

The first four of the six core human needs are defined as the needs of the personality or achievement. They are:

1. Certainty – The need for safety, stability, security, comfort, order, predictability, control, and consistency.

2. Uncertainty or Variety – The need for variety, surprise, challenges, excitement, difference, adventure, change, and novelty.

These first two needs, *certainty* and *variety*, work with each other (i.e. as a paradox). If there is an imbalance in one need, such as too much certainty, you could experience boredom and crave adventure. If you have too much uncertainty, you may feel that your life is out of control.

3. Significance – The need to have meaning, special, pride, needed, wanted, sense of importance, and be worthy of love.

4. Love and Connection – The need for communication, unified, approval, and attachment – to feel connected with, intimate with, and loved by other human beings.

Significance and love and connection are also paradoxes. If you spend too much time gaining significance, you may have trouble finding deep intimate relationships that thrive on love and connection.

Needs of the Spirit

The final two needs are defined as the needs of the spirit and provide the structure for fulfillment and happiness. The needs of the spirit are:

5. Growth – The need for constant emotional, intellectual, and spiritual development.

6. Contribution – The need to give beyond ourselves, give, care, protect, and serve others.

Each day we fulfill these core needs – either in a constructive, resourceful way, a neutral way, or in a destructive, unresourceful way. Once we develop greater awareness around the six core human needs and why we do what we do, we can then consider other ways to meet these needs in a more resourceful way and create inner peace and harmony with our lives.

— BALANCE THE TIME YOU FOCUS ON FULFILLING EACH OF YOUR 6 HUMAN NEEDS —

Finding out what your top core needs are in a relationship will give you more understanding of yourself and your partner. For example, if your number one core need is *significance* and your partner's is *growth,* then you both will need to be more open in your communication together, so you can start getting that need met from one another. It's also important to find out what your children's top core needs are as well. Once you know you can create deeper rapport and connections, you will feel more valued in your core needs and they will as well. If you would like to learn more about this and make some powerful changes in your life fast, I highly recommend attending Tony Robbins's seminars Unleash the Power Within and Date with Destiny.

Communication Code 13

THE POWER OF ANCHORING

What is anchoring?

Anchoring is an internal process of the mind that uses an external stimulus, such as a sound, a picture, a touch, smell, or taste, that triggers a consistent response in you or someone else. We learn by making connections and associations.

When a stimulus is anchored into your mind or body, you react without thinking. This can be useful or painful. When you visit your grandparents you feel like a child again. Or the smell of fresh-baked cookies may remind you of home. Those are positive anchors. Other anchors have a negative or painful effect. Can you think of someone who, whenever you see them, you feel uncomfortable? Often, symptoms of Post Traumatic Stress Disorder (PTSD) are due to negative sound anchors. The sound of car backfiring may remind a former soldier of gunshots and all of the sudden he feels like he's back in combat.

Anchors are built by repetition and association.

The Russian scientist, Ivan Pavlov, conditioned his dogs by ringing a bell every time he fed them. The dogs became anchored to the sound of the bell and their mouths would begin to salivate each time they heard a bell ring. It is a stimulus response to the brain.

Anchors Can Occur in Every Channel

Visual anchors – stopping at a red light, colors that affect our mood, a photo of someone that brings up memories and feelings.

Auditory anchors – songs that take you back to a given time and place, a police siren, a loved one's voice, a certain tone your mother or father uses, *sssh* for silence.

Kinesthetic anchors – a warm hug, the feel of soft grass on your feet from your childhood backyard, head scratches when you get your hair washed.

Olfactory anchors – fresh apple pie that reminds you of your mother, smell of a campfire.

Gustatory anchors – taste of watermelon that reminds you of summer time, bubblegum that takes your mind back to when you were a kid.

Most anchors are developed accidentally when something in the environment is associated with a given state. A horse jumps up and frightens a person, and they feel frightened every time they see a horse. Or someone is pushed in the deep end of a pool without knowing how to swim. The fear is very real every time that person thinks of swimming or getting near a horse. We can overcome any negative emotional anchor by associating something positive over and over again, and that will collapse that negative anchor. The most common use of anchoring is to access resources, feelings, and states when you want them. Replacing unwanted feelings and thoughts with desirable ones is freedom indeed.

We also become anchored in our relationships. How our partners look at us will induce a certain feeling or response immediately. A certain tone of voice or sigh can trigger our emotions quickly. When you can recognize what your negative anchors are toward your partner, then you can begin to become more conscious and aware of how to stop reacting negatively to them and start replacing negative triggers with positive, more effective emotions. Whether it be a certain look or expression, or a way they speak to you that reminds you of the way your parents spoke to you, most negative anchors are from the past, usually during your childhood, and are unconscious. To see how to set positive anchors and collapse negative anchors, you can find many videos on "NLP anchoring techniques" on YouTube.

One of my favorite anchoring techniques, that I will share is called **Stuck to Clear**.

This powerful technique is a way to become clear

in many areas of your life whenever you are feeling stuck. Whether it be stuck in traffic, feeling stuck in a relationship, or stuck in a situation that you're not sure how to get out of.

When we are stuck we usually become confused. Most of us keep looping over and over stuck, confused, stuck, confused. The reason we are stuck and confused is because we are *missing something*. Missing some kind of information. For instance, if you have lost something like your car keys, your mind can become stuck, confused, and now you are literally missing something. Whatever the situation may be, this one process can help you get clearer much faster.

The first step is recognize that you're stuck. The second step, acknowledge that you're confused. Third, notice you are missing something. In order to get clear you have to get to the fourth step. Can you think of what this next step could be? What is that one thing that could possibly get your mind moving towards clear?

In order to get *clear* you must go to *curiosity* first. The state of being curious moves your mind out of missing something. Curiosity directs the mind toward seeking answers and ultimately getting you in the state you want to be: *clear, alert,* and *moving again*. How do you set Stuck-to-Clear anchors so you can move out of stuck-ness quickly, you may be wondering? You program each of the five anchors (stuck, confused, missing something, curiosity, and clear) into the knuckles of your hand. This gives you "buttons" you can push to move your mind from feeling stuck to being clear. Here is the protocol:

1. Stuck - Think of a time when you felt stuck. Maybe it was while you were stuck in traffic or struggled to loosen a jar lid that was on too tight. Any memory will do. The key is to find a good memory to recreate the state you were in when you were absolutely stuck. Now, close your eyes, remember that incident, and see everything you saw when you were stuck. Visualize it with as much details as possible, as if you are actually there. Hear and feel everything you heard and felt when you were stuck. Feel the frustration. At that moment, make a fist with your left hand and touch the top of your thumb knuckle with your right finger and hold it down for 30 seconds while you're still remembering that time when you were stuck. You are setting your first anchor. Then after 30 seconds release your finger and take a deep breath.

2. Confused - Think of a time when you were confused. Same thing—see, hear, and feel a time when you were really confused. Then touch your second knuckle—your index finger knuckle—and hold that anchor for 30 seconds while you're thinking of that time you were confused. Then release it and relax a moment.

3. Missing Something - Think of a time when you were missing something. Maybe you lost your keys or sunglasses or realized you arrived somewhere without something important you meant to bring. Now, see, hear and really feel that time when you were missing something. Touch your third (middle) knuckle and hold down pressure for 30 seconds. You are only touching and anchoring one knuckle at a time with each memory. You are anchoring those feelings into your knuckles and it is easy to do on your own.

4. Curiosity - Then think of a time when you were super curious about something. This is really important. A time when you received a present and wondered what was inside the box, or you wondered how someone kissed or what their touch might feel like. Use anything that peeks your curiosity to its highest level. The number one curiosity is sexual curiosity. So if you're curious what someone would be like as a lover or how someone looks in their sexy birthday suit, then that would be a powerful curiosity anchor. Amplify those feelings then touch your fourth knuckle and press down and hold for 30 seconds. You have now anchored 4 out of 5 states on each knuckle.

5. Clear - The last anchor you set is *clear*. Remember a time when you knew that you knew something, or something that you absolutely know that you know. It can be as simple as you know what your name is. You know your phone number. You know that the sun rises. Just pick something you were 100 percent clear that you knew. Then touch your thumb knuckle now and hold it for 30 seconds as you keep thinking of that time when you were totally clear and knew that you knew. Now let go of the fifth anchor and take a deep breath.

Wait a few seconds, then go back to your first anchor of being stuck and touch the exact same knuckle as before and hold it. This time keep holding it as you keep your finger pressed down on the first knuckle, touch the second knuckle, *confused*. While still holding your fingers down on anchors one and two, now press your third finger to number three anchor (middle knuckle) of *missing something* and hold it down as well. Keeping the first three fingers held down, then press the number four *curiosity* anchor and hold. You should now have four of your right fingers pressed down on the first four of your left knuckles. Finally, with your pinky, press the number five knuckle, your *clear* anchor.

I usually take my right hand and do the anchoring on my left hand, but do what feels comfortable. One finger for each knuckle. Think of your knuckles as buttons and each one you press fires off a different anchor in sequential order. This sends a signal to the brain to move your mind through the process of being stuck to unstuck (clear). It's very effective.

After holding all five anchors for 30 seconds, you will release one finger at a time in the same order that you placed them. Your Stuck-to-Clear anchors are set and ready to use the next time you feel stuck or confused. When you find yourself in either of these states, pause a moment and push your anchored knuckles in the order that you set them. Your mind will shorten the time it takes when you're stuck or confused. Your curious mind will immediately begin to search and find an opening or clearing with whatever you're going through. To strengthen the anchors, I recommend going through this process of anchoring your knuckles once every day for 21 days. It only takes a few minutes. You can also re-activate your knuckle anchors again and again.

Eventually, you can reach the point that simply thinking or saying the words "Stuck to Clear" will quickly move you to clear. This is very useful when looking for a parking spot. I will say out loud "Stuck to Clear" and within seconds I will find a place to park. I will also go into curiosity and ask, "I wonder if I can find a place to park today," and right away, I find a space close to the store. This may seem like magic, but this works on many situations—finding parking spots, finding your keys, going from being stuck in traffic to moving "in the flow" again, or unsticking a relationship you may feel is stuck. Remember to get curious, begin to wonder what the solution is, and say to yourself or out loud "STUCK to CLEAR." You will shorten the time between stuck, confused, missing something, curiosity, and get yourself to clear faster than you can imagine.

Communication Code 14

STOP GETTING DEFENSIVE

Defensiveness shuts down communication. If you are in a relationship with someone who is defensive then you know how frustrating it can be. It's difficult to communicate without fearing you are going to trigger a reaction. So you walk on egg shells around that person in order to keep the peace. This doesn't make for a healthy relationship.

Why do some people have this automatic emotional defensive response and others don't?

Well, we all have it. The difference is that each person has their own way they deal with stress. In those instances of defense our fight-or-flight mode is activated and we unconsciously want to protect ourself, shut down, fight, or flee the situation. You may wonder why you can't get over it. Your partner may be thinking you are being oppositional, difficult, or just strong willed. This is usually not the case.

Getting defensive is an unconscious, automatic response when perceiving danger. Situations that we have learned that are threatening trigger that danger state before we are even aware of it. Going into fight-or-flight is instinctual, not intentional.

There is another way. Defensiveness can be managed. You must first recognize that you are more sensitive and defensive than most people. It's not to make you wrong in any way, it's to make you more aware.

— ONCE YOU CAN OWN YOUR DEFENSIVENESS, THEN IT DOESN'T OWN YOU. —

What does that mean? If you don't have a clue that you respond in a defensive manner then it is unlikely for you to change your behavior. How do you know if you're being defensive? If you are feeling tight in your body or a sense that you are being criticized, rejected, attacked, or judged... If you notice you feel this way when you're around many people in your life other than your partner, such as friends, family, and co-workers... Then you know the trigger of defensiveness is something in you that needs to be looked at and healed.

Once you learn to manage your own inner critic, you are less likely to be so defensive. You begin to listen with a different filter. Stop taking things so personally, and instead of reacting, ask questions and get curious. What I've learned is most people that are defensive are really hard on themselves. I can tell you firsthand that I used to be defensive and very reactive until I understood that I was feeling judged and criticized. I was judging and being so hard on myself as well. If you come from a family that was hard on you then most likely you will continue to be hard on yourself. Sometimes it's not even conscious. You will have a hard time getting your needs met if you keep reacting and responding in a defensive way.

A Few Things to Help Stop Being So Defensive

Start by being gentle with yourself, especially how you are speaking and what you are saying to yourself. Becoming aware of when you start getting defensive is the key in learning how to do something to change it. Acknowledge what is happening and let your partner know that you are getting defensive. Tell them you need to take a moment to calm down so you can hear what they're saying without reacting. Breathe, and stop talking so you can re-center yourself. This creates time and space needed for you to identify and understand what you're really feeling. Also, notice was there someone in your family who triggered you like this. In other words, is this a familiar pattern for you? Did your partner use the same angry tone as your mother or look at you intensely like your father? Recognizing this familiar pattern will sometimes take the charge out of your defensiveness when you can uncover the truth that is underneath your reaction.

Does your partner remind you of one of your parents? I found that was usually the case in many of my relationships. Seeing this was a pattern, and an emotional trigger, that I brought into my relationships was extremely healing and it helped me understand and control my defensiveness. Also, stop making excuses when you get defensive. And stop blaming the other person for your feelings and reactions. That person probably didn't install those emotional triggers. Most likely, you brought them into the relationship, so take responsibility for your triggers and own them. Then you can gain power over them and reduce the need to get defensive.

Remember that you are the only one who can manage your own emotional state. No one is responsible for your feelings. No one can be right one hundred percent of the time. Even though you would like to be. There are times when you need to recognize that the other person is correct in what they are saying or observing. Give yourself permission to be wrong sometimes without getting defensive. Also give permission to others to be wrong as well. Then you're accepting the fact that it's okay to not be right all the time. Once you can make peace with being wrong then you will stop getting so defensive. Also, if you can look at the bigger picture in those moments when you are being defensive, you can realize that, in the long run, it won't bring you closer to your partner. By being able to stop yourself from reacting in that negative way, you can come up with a healthier and more positive response.

Communication Code 15

STOP BLAMING OTHERS

Most of us define blame as holding others accountable for our mistakes or misfortunes. Some people blame their parent, teachers, spouses, past relationships, disadvantages, or other hardships for their lack of success or unhappiness.

To blame others for your unhappiness is to keep you stuck in being a victim. It may seem easier to blame others for your life, but the real truth is that you're avoiding taking responsibility. Most people who play the victim are getting something positive out of it. It usually isn't conscious. A person who plays the victim could be getting attention, sympathy, or some other benefit that they are not aware of.

Pointing the finger at someone else and justifying why you are blaming will keep you in a powerless state of victimhood. The only thing blame does is keep the focus off you when you're looking for a reason to explain your anger, frustration, or unhappiness. It's time to stop using other people as the scapegoat in your life. It's time now to start taking responsibility and take your power back. What I've learned is that when people blame it's because somewhere they are not happy in their own lives. Or that they feel like they are at fault or may be wrong in some way.

Letting go of blame doesn't make you wrong or invalidate whatever you're feeling. Nor does it mean that people in your life aren't difficult or problematic. Letting go of blame and taking responsibility means you get to reclaim your freedom and power in a way that doesn't keep you playing the victim.

I worked with a couple where the husband constantly was blaming everyone for his problems, most of all his wife. He would blame her if he was late to work because she didn't set the alarm earlier. He blamed her for pretty much everything that was going wrong in his life. This man could not take responsibility for anything. They were on the verge of divorce when I stepped in. After working with them for many hours, we discovered that this man had a father that was such a perfectionist. The father blamed him for everything that went wrong when he was a child. He was filled with anxiety and didn't realize how it had been affecting him. We also uncovered that if he was ever wrong he was criticized, shamed, blamed, and ultimately punished. So this man could never be wrong. He made it mean that he was stupid, worthless, and that he was unlovable. None of this was conscious or obviously true. When he realized how much this impacted his life he broke down in tears. To see this man have a breakthrough was very powerful! He was afraid of taking responsibility because of what had happened in his childhood. After the sessions were complete this man had transformed completely. The wife had much more understanding and compassion for him, and he began to have it for himself as well. He was no longer a victim or behaving like a little boy who wasn't good enough. He took his power back and started taking responsibility for his life. The blaming stopped. After doing this work he noticed that his anxiety had completely disappeared. To be free from anxiety has given him such freedom and peace.

— IT TAKES A BIG PERSON TO ADMIT WHEN THEY HAVE MADE A MISTAKE, AND AN EVEN A BIGGER PERSON TO WORK ON THEMSELVES AND STOP PLAYING THE BLAME GAME. —

Another thing that couples do that keeps the blame game going is keeping score with each other, or simply put, "tit for tat." It describes the underlying power struggle that exists in most relationships. A competition in which one person is trying to prove to the other that they have done more, contributed more, or that their life has been harder for them more than their partner's. One person will say, "Look at everything I have done for you! Now, you owe me and you should do this or that for me!" Unfortunately, the other person doesn't see it the same way. There is this constant giant scoreboard that is going on in each of their minds assessing the value of what has been done.

I recently worked with a couple where the wife is a stay-at-home mom and the husband is gone working all day. She feels that her job is very stressful taking care of the baby, doing all of the house chores and having dinner prepared for her husband. Now, from the husband's perspective, her job is a piece of cake and doesn't compare to the stress and pressure of his job. So, when they get together they each want support, sympathy, and validation from the other, but they usually don't get it because they are both upset. Resentment has already built up from feeling that they each have had such a hard day. There was no understanding, compassion, or validation happening from either them. Neither one was willing to acknowledge the struggles or stressfulness of the other. The husband wanted to be right and win. He wanted her to acknowledge that he had it way harder than her. The wife needed the same thing. You can see their predicament. Holding on to being right and keeping score, tit for tat, was a contest with no winners.

I suggested that if they would just be willing to give each other encouragement, validation, and understanding that the tension and struggle would dissipate. Fortunately, they were on the same team in regards to overcoming their issue. They both aimed to work together to build a happy family for their baby and with each other. The more we uncovered, the more they admitted to doing this tit-for-tat behavior throughout their relationship.

The biggest problem with this tit-for-tat mindset is that it's nearly impossible to calculate the worth of each person's actions and behavior. So stop keeping score. If the relationships feels out of balance, then it's time to sit down and have a conversation about it. Set boundaries and remember that when you're in a healthy relationship, things just flow naturally, without the need for scorekeeping. You give because you love the person, and they do the same. Not because you're expecting something in return. It's okay to want to receive back. Take responsibility and ask for what you need so you can begin to create the balance once again with your partner.

Because this couple had the courage to be honest and acknowledge what they were doing. They were able to really commit to stopping this behavior. Becoming aware is the first step in healing and being willing to get help is second. The positive rewards that working together brings are well worth it!

Communication Code 16

REDUCE ANXIETY

Sometimes a person has deeper issues that affect their ability to communicate and create harmony in their relationships. They may be suffering from some form of anxiety disorder. Anxiety can be a serious health condition. I am not a doctor nor can I prescribe anything for it. If you suffer from anxiety then you know how it can affect your life. It can be difficult to have a simple conversation with someone or to even go to the grocery store. This chapter is to share with you what I did to help myself get through my own intense, and sometimes overwhelming, anxiety. Here I give techniques that I used that were helpful when dealing with this issue. To understand better, it's important to know that there are many types of anxiety disorders? Some types develop and remain long-term. Many start in childhood and last into adulthood, if treatment has not been sought.

A list of anxiety disorders:

Agoraphobia – a fear of being in a public place where escape would be embarrassing or difficult. This is particularly prevalent when a person fears they may have a panic attack.

Anxiety due to a general medical condition – this disorder can be short or long-term, depending on the medical condition. Anxiety often develops in relation to illnesses like heart conditions.

Generalized Anxiety Disorder (GAD) – anxiety symptoms occur in multiple environments and are due to multiple objects or situations. Anxiety symptoms may not have a known cause.

Obsessive-Compulsive Disorder (OCD) – anxiety symptoms are in the form of intrusive, obsessive thoughts and compulsive behaviors (or mental acts). OCD is considered a chronic type of anxiety disorder.

Panic Disorder – consists of severe, immediate anxiety symptoms (a panic attack) due to a variety of causes, as well as the worry over having another panic attack.

Post Traumatic Stress Disorder (PTSD) – anxiety symptoms that occur after a trauma. These are long-term in nature.

Social Phobia, also referred to as Social Anxiety Disorder (SAD) – anxiety symptoms occur in social or performance situations and stem from the fear of being humiliated or embarrassed.

Specific Phobia (also known as a simple phobia) – anxiety symptoms occur around a specific object or situation which results in avoidance. Fear of snakes, spiders, heights, or the water, are a few examples of specific phobias.

There are no quick fixes when it comes to anxiety. Triggers that cause anxiety can be deeply rooted in the mind and body, or be a byproduct of the person's conditioning or belief system. There are ways to alleviate anxiety and improve the quality of your life. If you're in a relationship with someone who has anxiety, this chapter could help you both. If you are the one suffering, make sure that you have a solid support system in place—family members, friends, or a therapist that you can call whenever the anxiety starts. There are different levels and degrees of anxiety. It can start as a feeling of nervousness and begin to escalate to a full-blown panic attack.

I used to have full-blown panic attacks when I was a child, all the way up into my twenties. I would literally shake and sometimes get a horrible migraine because the anxiety was too overwhelming. My mother didn't know what to do and didn't know what was happening. So she would take me to the hospital and doctors would use medication to sedate me until I eventually calmed down or passed out. They didn't know much back then about anxiety attacks, unfortunately. Sometimes my panic attacks would get triggered without a warning of any kind. This overwhelming sense of fear and dread would take over, my heart would be pounding, my body shaking, and sometimes I felt like I was going to die.

It was terrifying, to say the least. As I got older I could feel when the panic attacks were coming on, and if I were home, I would get a cold towel and place it on the back of my neck and forehead. I would begin to breathe, and sometimes that would help. Sometimes I would take a walk and notice that the anxiety would dissipate faster.

If you have anxiety get your body moving. Walking, stretching, or any kind of light exercise can be effective temporarily. It releases endorphins and will start calming your body down immediately. Remind yourself to redirect the energy, because when the anxiety happens you can feel completely stuck and overwhelmed. I've found that movement is one of the best things you can do.

Breathing deeply is a key to controlling anxiety. When a person is feeling anxious, they breathe high in their chest. Their breathing is typically shallow. Under extreme cases it can turn into hyperventilating. To reduce this state of anxiety, take long deep breaths all the way down into your belly. Then slowly exhale. Repeat slow, deep inhaling and exhaling for several minutes. This will help you get centered.

What also helped me was if someone would gently touch or hold me, then I would start to calm down quicker. Some people don't like to be touched, so make sure to ask them what they need. If you're the one who suffers from anxiety, sometimes you're not in a place to talk, so it's always good to talk about things that help before you have an attack. Then your partner will be more prepared to help you get through it when it happens. Another thing I learned that helped with anxiety was to laugh. We know anxiety is no laughing matter, but if you even fake laugh it will release dopamine, a brain chemical associated with pleasure. Watching a funny movie will reduce stress, as well, and can help reduce anxiety.

If you're with your partner, let them know what's going on, so they can support you. What most people who suffer from anxiety need is validation. I know I did. If you are the one supporting a loved one who suffers from anxiety, it helps to acknowledge that they are suffering and for their partner to be present and gentle with them as much as possible. And to reassure them that you are there to help in any way. Talk softly and let them know that they are safe and continue reassuring them that they are not alone. Compassion, comfort, and understanding will help your partner have relief soon.

How I Gained Power Over My Anxiety

In my twenties, I started working on myself and uncovered how I worried so much as a child. My mother was sick often and I was terrified that she would die. I knew I was constantly scared and worried about my mother's health, but I had no conscious idea that most of my anxiety stemmed from that. I cleared so much of the fear and worry out of my mind and body that finally the panic attacks stopped completely. I still will feel anxious at times but it only lasts a few minutes, because I use many different techniques to help the anxiousness go away.

A fast an easy technique to help with anxiety is called Emotional Freedom Technique. EFT uses tapping different points on your body in a specific order that will lessen anxiety quickly. There are many YouTube videos that can teach you how to do EFT. The tapping technique usually takes less than 5 minutes to do on yourself. Also, I will listen to a hypnosis video at night or in the morning. There are many to choose from on YouTube as well. One of my favorites is "Sleep and Anxiety" by Michael Sealey. Make sure you put your earphones on and give yourself time to relax and enjoy this process. I would recommend listening to the hypnosis video once a day for at least 21 days in a row. It's very helpful and really relaxing too.

Using aromatherapy is another method. I will also use a drop of lavender oil on my temples and stomach, as well, if I feel any kind of anxiety coming on. Massage therapy is extremely helpful too. I never took any medication as an adult for anxiety. There are many natural ways that can help, if you choose. Whatever you choose, make sure you are under a doctor's supervision.

Communication Code 17

FACE YOUR SHADOW

The shadow is a psychological term for everything that we can't see in ourselves. It is the negative emotions hidden from our consciousness like rage, greed, jealousy, selfishness, or any dark parts that we won't acknowledge in ourselves. The shadow is the disowned self, the parts inside that we deny, make wrong, bad, or perceive as unacceptable. Although we may deny or repress these negative emotions in our attempt to cast them out, we never get rid of them because they are part of our unconscious.

Whatever negative qualities or traits you deny in yourself, you will usually see it in another person. It is called projection. We project onto others things that are hidden or buried within us. If someone irritates you because they are demanding or impatient, you will usually find that sometimes you too have been demanding or impatient as well. In other words:

— IF YOU SPOT IT, YOU GOT IT. —

If you are triggered it's because, somewhere inside, you are doing the same thing or have done it, or it wouldn't have even bothered you at all. It would be a good time to own your demanding and impatient parts of yourself. Then it doesn't own you and you're less likely to be irritated or triggered.

Most of the time we are not consciously aware that we are projecting. These projections can distort reality, especially how we view ourselves and how we are in our relationships and in the world. No one enjoys looking at their flaws or our so called weaknesses. Being willing to face and explore our shadow sides gives us a tremendous opportunity for growth and development. When you can accept your own shadow, then it will be easier to accept someone else's. It will also be easier to communicate with others, because you won't be triggered or bothered in the same way, once you've accepted those shadow sides of yourself. You will have more compassion, understanding, and clarity for others, because you now are aware of your shadow parts.

This shadow work changed the course of my life in such a powerful and profound way! When I began to face my shadow it wasn't a pretty sight, I must confess. I had gone to many seminars and learned different processes to get in touch with my darker self. Here is one of the many stories that helped transform my life.

When I was a little girl I became cross-eyed at eight-months-old, because of being a preemie and having many health issues. I had little glasses strapped to my baby head and as I grew, I really hated those glasses. By the time I was three, I would take my glasses off, and out of sheer anger and rage, I would snap them right in half right in front of my mother. She would punish me and tape my glasses back together and make me wear the broken ones. I remember hearing her calling me the b-word to my father many times but I didn't know what it meant. This happened on a regular basis. I was incorrigible, to say the least. I even remember one time after I broke my ugly taped glasses that I went to the backyard, dug a hole, and buried them. I must have been four at that time. When my mother came home from work and asked where my glasses were, I looked at her and told her the dog stole them and ran off with them. Once again, I was punished and eventually had to go outside and dig up those hideous glasses.

As you can imagine, life as a cross-eyed little girl with glasses was no fun at all. I finally stopped breaking my glasses when I started school, because there was no way I was going to school wearing ugly taped glasses. I had learned my lesson.

When I was eleven, we were told that I could have surgery on both eyes to correct them. It was the happiest news of my life! That is, until my siblings started teasing and scaring me before the surgery, saying that they had to take my eyeballs out and lay them on my cheeks to fix them. Something that was supposed to be the happiest time in my life turned into a total horror show. I was now terrified. My parents assured me that this wasn't true and that my siblings were just teasing. It was a cruel joke and I wasn't laughing.

The surgery was a total success and my eyes were now straight and perfect. Within a year, I no longer had to wear those horrible glasses. I was still really angry with my siblings, especially after I found out that the surgeons did have to take my eyes out to cut the muscles in order to fix them. I argued, fought, and was such a brat to my family so much that they all began to call me the b-word again. Now I knew what that word meant and I didn't care. So I had thought.

Years later, I went to a seminar on healing the shadow. I didn't even know what the shadow was. I just knew I had to go and attend this seminar. The teachers wanted us to think of a few words that, if people would call you this word, then you would get triggered—become angry, sad, or feel any negative emotions that would arise in you. Of course, you know what my trigger word was. I would become enraged if anyone called me the b-word. I mean I hated this word! During the seminar, I had to get into a small group with strangers and say the word out loud. Not only share this vile word but I had to look at these people and say, "I am a bitch!"

I remember thinking, *Oh, hell no there is no way I'm going to say that!*

However, this was the exercise I had to do if I wanted to stay in this training. Then, to help me face my shadow, the other people in the group would look at me and say, "You are such a bitch!" Seriously, I couldn't do it. And what was even worse was that I was the one who chose to go first, because I obviously didn't know what I was getting myself into. I reluctantly agreed to lead the exercise. We had to go back and forth and I would say, "I am a bitch," and then the other people in the group would say "You are a bitch." Over and over this process went. I was so angry at first. Saying those words physically hurt my body. They hurt my ears too, grating on my nerves. There was no relief in sight. Until one woman looked at me with such compassion in her eyes and said those words again. All of a sudden it hit me like a bolt of lightning.

"I am such a bitch! I am such a bitch! I am such a total bitch!"

Oh my gosh, I broke down and started to cry. I was holding on to so much resentment and rage toward my family because of what had happened in my childhood. I couldn't believe it! I was being a total bitch! The more I cried and released, the easier it was to say those words. Until I eventually started to laugh. Those words didn't own me anymore! It was such an empowering feeling! There was no more charge on it at all!

— EITHER YOU OWN WHAT'S HIDDEN IN YOUR SHADOW OR IT OWNS YOU. —

I called a few of my family members and apologized for hanging on to all the resentment and told them they were right. I had been such a bitch to them. They said they were so sorry too and that they never meant to hurt my feelings. They were just kids back then too. This was the first step in facing one of my shadow parts. Just because I had a bitch part didn't mean my whole being was a bitch. It doesn't negate all the good that you are when you own a side of your shadow. This work brought such an inner healing, strength, and balance to my life, because now I could own those negative things inside myself that I couldn't look at before. It also meant that I didn't have to continue being a bitch. I could change that aspect of my shadow and be nicer to people more often.

Once you understand that we all have dark shadow parts and it doesn't negate any of the positive good parts of us either, it's very healing and transforming. When you own your negative parts then they have no charge on you anymore. And you will have no more reactions, when people call you the words that used to trigger you.

If you want to attempt to understand your shadow, make sure you are centered, calm, and in a safe environment. The ability to reflect and observe your behaviors, thoughts, and feelings will help you recognize your shadow. To be honest with yourself takes a lot of courage when dealing with your shadow sides. The more you come to terms with your unowned parts, the more comfortable you will start to be. Another way to become aware of your shadow is to pay attention to your emotional triggers and reactions toward others. You can train yourself to be aware of your shadow when you notice you're having a negative emotional response. You can also write down a few words that if someone called you these things you would be upset or triggered in some way. Then see if you can own that shadow part by saying it to yourself or out loud. If people call you a jerk and it triggers you, then own that part by saying, "I am a jerk. I am a jerk. I AM a jerk." Or if you've been accused of being selfish and that ruffles your feathers, say to yourself, "I am selfish. I am selfish. I AM selfish." Then imagine someone saying it back to you, or even better, have a friend or life coach repeat the statement back to you. Accepting your shadow part can be very empowering. Once you own that part, when someone labels you as that word, it will no longer have a charge. Remember that stating your shadow part doesn't negate all the positive, good, and wonderful parts of you just because you are looking at those darker sides of yourself.

Next, see if you can identify the positive reason why you have that shadow part. A person who is sometimes a jerk may be behaving this way to protect themselves from being bullied. It may be a form of setting boundaries. Or deep down, they're afraid you'll discover they are very sensitive, so they've shielded themselves with a prickly personality. They could have also been raised by a jerk parent and that's how they learned to operate in the world. They didn't even know they were being a jerk until others pointed it out. A person who is sometimes selfish might be needing to take care of their personal needs first before they can be emotionally centered enough to support others. Or they want to maintain some autonomy so they aren't losing themselves in their relationships. Identifying the positive reason behind your shadow part will help you gain insight as to why you sometimes behave that way.

The final part of the process in the shadow work is to acknowledge the opposite of your shadow. For instance, after I owned my bitch side, I then owned my positive sides and said, "I am kind and caring." Keep saying the phrase to yourself until you start to feel it going inside of you. Sometimes it can be harder to own the positive parts of yourself if you're struggling with your self-esteem or if you didn't get a lot of praise, recognition, or acknowledgement as a child. This exercise can be very useful in your relationship as well, because you both can say to each other the positive things you see in one another, and then you will begin to feel more connection, appreciation, and respect. I call that "watering your partner," using the metaphor of watering plants in a garden, to give your partner the nourishment we all need.

Communication Code 18

WATER YOUR PARTNER AND YOURSELF

It's obvious that we all need praise, appreciation, and respect in our relationships. This has been one of the constant complaints I've heard from couples, as I've mentioned before. They're not feeling appreciated, respected, or heard in a way that is nourishing to the relationship. This chapter is to remind you of simple and effective ways to "water" or nourish your relationship with respect and appreciation, and most of all, how to water yourself.

We all may crave compliments, but it's not because we're needy or attention seeking. It's because some of us hardly get them. Compliments make people happy, even more so when it's from the person we love. When coming from a genuine, authentic, and honest place, a compliment can brighten your entire day and stay with you for weeks.

— COMPLIMENTS ARE THE FUNDAMENTAL BUILDING BLOCKS OF INTIMACY. —

They build connection and help your partner feel more noticed, seen, and loved. If you tend to need more compliments than your partner, then it's time to speak up.

Have you ever noticed that there will be one person in the relationship that may not compliment as much and may not feel comfortable giving or receiving them?

If this is an issue in your relationship, then know that there is work to be done. When someone is feeling uncomfortable giving or receiving compliments, it usually has to do with their own self-esteem. It could be because they didn't get them growing up, or if they were shy and self-conscious it was harder to express them. If this is your issue, practice giving compliments to yourself. Find some things you like about yourself, positive traits and qualities that you know you have, and look in the mirror and praise your best traits to yourself or out loud. You may feel silly or uncomfortable at first, keep complimenting yourself anyway until you can smile and feel it getting easier and feel it going inside of you. This is how you begin to water yourself.

When it comes to complimenting your partner, do the same thing as you did for yourself. Express those positive qualities you like about them. Remind them of all the things that made you fall in love with them in the beginning. Even if that was years ago. There are many different variations of compliments you can use to remind you and your partner what makes you feel more love, respect, and appreciation in your relationship.

Compliments That Acknowledge Your Efforts

Show your partner that you appreciate the little things they do for you. Even the smallest things will make a difference. Cooking, doing the dishes, washing the car, mowing the lawn, or folding the clothes, to name a few. What's important is that you recognize each other for the effort. Expressing it to each other out loud will make each of you want to do it more. I've had many clients say that the reason they stopped doing the small things was because they didn't feel valued or appreciated. I had the other partner say that they thought he or she knew that they were appreciated. It takes only a few seconds of your life to speak up and give the praise and acknowledgment that you both need. Start today by remembering to compliment the small stuff too.

Compliments of Support

Letting your partner know that you believe in him or her and that you have their back is one of the most important things you can do in a relationship. It shows loyalty, love, and honoring your partner when you support each other. It also will help you feel more confident and a sense that you can accomplish anything with that kind of constant support and acknowledgment. Many of my male clients have shared that whenever they feel support from their partner, it makes life much easier and they feel more respected. Especially when it comes to their job or when they provide for their partner and family. During coaching sessions, women clients share that they feel more love when their partners acknowledge them and give support. When partners offer each other compliments of support, everyone benefits. Ask questions to find out how to support each other more and watch your relationship blossom.

Compliments of Respect

This seems to be number one with men. Respect equals love to many men. They tend to need to feel respected in the relationship more. Women need it as well; they just usually don't equate respect with love in the same way. How do you show respect with your partner? One way to compliment is to let them know how proud you are of them and tell them the reasons why you have so much respect for them. Respect for what he does, for what he knows, and how he treats you. The men I've worked with confess that it is such a turn on for them when they know how much they are respected by their partner. They want to keep contributing to the relationship and they feel more loved. Women tend to feel more secure and loved when they feel respected by their partner. When respect is present the quality of the relationship improves, and the connection between you grows deeper and stronger.

Compliments of Appearance

Every person, regardless of gender, likes knowing that their partner finds them aesthetically pleasing. Complimenting your partner's body and appearance is one way to do so. Even though women tend to be more critical about their body and need more reassurance than men, know that men have their own insecurities going on when it comes to their physical appearance too. Be specific when complimenting. Especially when it comes to someone's looks. Saying you're beautiful or handsome is great, it's even better to give specific details. For example, "You're eyes look so gorgeous in that dress," or "That shirt really shows off your muscles and it's such a turn on." For those on the receiving end, never discount or invalidate a compliment. Compliments are little gifts of love. The only way to receive a compliment is graciously with a smile. The positive energy that compliments create can transform any relationship. If you want the magic back in your relationships, then start watering and complimenting the people in your life. The more we take notice and become more aware and conscious of the good that people bring to our world, the more we cultivate those qualities within ourselves.

Compliments of Desire

If you want to spice up your romantic relationships, then it's time to bring more compliments into the bedroom. It is important to know what your partner likes to hear in bed. Being more specific and less general with your compliments goes along way when it comes to what you're desiring. For instance, telling your partner that you like his/her moves in detail will definitely get the sparks flying. Let them know how you like to be touched—soft, slow, sensual, saying things like "Light feathery strokes make my body melt" and "I feel as though electricity is running through my entire body."

When your partner does those things that you love, make sure you shower them with praise and acknowledgment. Letting them know how it makes you feel in those moments, through words or making sounds, will be very effective and such a turn on. The power of touch allows the compliments to go in deeper. Those sweet compliments hold the key to even more pleasure.

Another exercise you can do with your partner is hold one another for at least 30 seconds (or even better several minutes), and gaze into each other's eyes, as you share intimate quality time together. This will take you to a deeper level of connection and intimacy. Then begin complimenting all the things you enjoyed and how it made you feel. This will create a little heaven on earth for you both.

These last chapters are the main ingredients to transform the quality of your relationships and take you to a whole new level of awareness, communication, connection, and depth. My hope is that you will utilize these tools, techniques, and information to create a healthier, happier, and new you in your relationships. Where you both feel loved, honored, and cherished. You now have more understanding, compassion, and tools to create the relationship of your dreams.

Communication Code 19

IDENTIFY STORY VS. MEANING

You know how we all have stories that happen in our lives? Then we have the meaning to those stories? A lot of the time we make something that happens mean more than what actually occurred. The two circles below illustrate the two ways of looking at an event. The circle on the left contains the *story* or *what happened*. On the right, you have the *meaning* or *interpretation* of what happened.

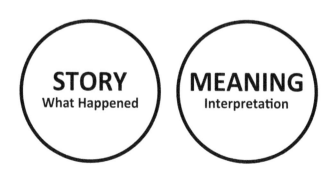

An example of a story would be a couple is having an outdoor wedding and a really bad thunderstorm blows in during the middle of it. Hard rain pours down, and strong winds and lightning send everyone running inside. That's what happened. An example of meaning would be that the bride may fear this storm is an omen warning her the marriage is doomed. Is that true? No, it's just an interpretation of an event. Any time something happens, it's important to see events only as they happened, just the facts. Avoid making events *mean* anything about yourself or another person.

This one distinction transformed my entire life in such a profound way that I wanted to share my personal story in order for you to get the impact of this distinction. Here is my story:

As I shared with you earlier, I was cross-eyed for the first eleven years of my life. When I was ten, my father came home drinking and took me out of bed and sat me on the high kitchen counter. He looked right in my eyes and started yelling, "Straighten your eyes! Straighten your eyes!"

I was really scared because I could smell the alcohol coming from his breath and he had never spoken like this to me before. Imagine my confusion as a little girl. I said, "What, how?"

All of a sudden he grabbed me, picked me up by my nightgown, lifted me in the air, and started shaking my body, screaming in my face and shouting, "You ugly cross-eyed little monkey!" Then he threw me on the floor and walked away without another word.

That's what happened. True story.

Now can you imagine what I made that one story mean? I made it mean I was worthless. It shattered me. How could anyone love me if that was what my daddy thought of me? Was it true that I was worthless and unlovable? No! That's what a ten-year-old girl made that event mean! The next day my father didn't remember anything. I told my mother what happened. He went to her and asked, "Why won't Donza speak to me?"

My mother was in shock! Went off on him and said, "You don't remember?" He didn't remember. He never even apologized at all. It was swept under the rug and never spoken about again.

Years later, I was in my late twenties and went to a seminar with over a hundred people. At that time I couldn't speak in public. The leader began to give this distinction about meaning verses story. I was in the second row and she asked, "Does anyone have a story they would like to share?" I put my hand on my cheek and she saw it and asked me to come up to the front, get the microphone, and share my story.

I responded, "Uh, no thank you."

"I want to hear your story," she said.

I was terrified to get up in front of people and speak, let alone share my dirty laundry with complete strangers! But I did. I told everyone the story of my father shaking me and calling me a cross-eyed little monkey and then throwing me to the floor. Feeling vulnerable in front of an audience, I shared how what happened made me feel so embarrassed and ashamed. I told them what I made that story mean, that I was worthless.

The seminar leader looked at me and said, "Wow, that's what happened when you were a little girl, and that's what you made it mean *then*. What can you make it mean *now*? You're not a little girl anymore."

I didn't understand at all. What was she talking about?

She said, "You made your father shaking you and yelling at you mean that you were worthless when you were ten. You're not ten anymore. What can you make what happened with your father mean now?"

Like a freight train, it hit me! Oh my gosh, it wasn't about me! It was about my dysfunctional drunken dad! I couldn't believe it! I broke down and started to cry in front of a hundred people. The seminar leader said, "You've been playing small your whole life and today it stops. It didn't mean that at all. That was what your little girl made it mean. Now you know what you have to do. You have to call your dad and clean this up with him."

"Why do I need to do that? He won't remember and he stopped drinking when I was twelve."

"It's not for him," she said. "It's for you."

I didn't know how I was going to share that abusive story with my father. But I did. I called him and told him what happened when I was ten.

"I'm so sorry, hun," he said. "I was a no good drunk." I couldn't believe those words actually came out of my dad's mouth! He actually apologized!

I broke down in tears again, and for the first time ever, I felt validated from my father. It was what I had been waiting for my whole life and needed so desperately. It was such an incredible healing that occurred that day. I no longer had to play small in my life anymore. I no longer made those stories mean anything negative about myself. There was a sense of freedom I had never felt before. My entire being truly transformed that day! Changing the meaning of my story was life altering and the most profound healing I'd ever had up to this point in my life.

We all have stories based on what happened to us in the past, and even now we're still making them mean something negative about ourselves that isn't the truth. Even more so in relationships. Once you can identify the meaning of a story, then ask yourself, *What did I make it mean in the past or what am I making it mean now?*

You can then change your perception and understanding and know that whatever happened didn't mean what you once thought or believed it meant about yourself. When you give your story a different meaning, you can begin to think differently about other old stories, your feelings, and yourself. Then start to heal in a way you never imagined possible.

We can't change our past, can we? We can only change how we feel about it. What's so great about the past is that it's over! This is so important to remember, it's worth repeating:

— WE CAN'T CHANGE OUR PAST. WE CAN ONLY CHANGE HOW WE FEEL ABOUT IT. —

When it comes to your relationship, ask questions to your partner about what they're making something that happened mean. For example, one of my clients would make dinner each night for her husband, and he would come home late on a regular basis. She made it mean that he didn't care about her or respect her. The husband was totally surprised that she made it mean that. His job sometimes required him to work late and he would call to let her know. But his wife still took it personally and made it mean something that wasn't true at all. It wasn't the husband's fault that she made his missing dinners mean that he didn't care or respect her. That was her interpretation, a fictional story she made up in her head. She didn't consciously even realize she was making it mean that.

When you ask questions to yourself and your partner about the meaning, you begin to discover the real truth that's going on now. You can reassure each other that what occurred in the past didn't mean what you both thought. Especially if your story is negative and causing hurt, pain, and frustration. The most important thing is to make sure you're now being more aware of the stories that you're telling yourself, and what you've made them mean.

Do this with your children as well. When something happens that upsets them, ask them, "What did you make that mean?" Ask them often because you have no idea what kids make up in their minds. I worked with a twelve-year-old girl that was failing math at school. I asked her to tell me what happened. She said the teacher came over and slammed a quiz paper on her desk and yelled in front of the class, "You are going to fail this class if you don't get your grades up!"

"What did you make it mean?" I asked the girl.

She looked down. "I made it mean I was stupid."

"Really?" I said. "Well, that's interesting. Aren't you one of the best horseback riders in the state?"

She looked up with big wide eyes. "Yes, I am."

"Aren't you an incredible piano player as well and a beautiful dancer too?"

She nodded.

"Could someone stupid learn all those things?"

All of a sudden her sweet blue eyes filled with tears and she said, "I'm not stupid! I'm not stupid!"

"No sweet girl, you're not stupid at all! What your teacher said doesn't mean that."

The girl broke down and cried so hard, repeating, "I'm not stupid! I'm not stupid!"

"No you're not stupid." I kept repeating and reassuring her.

Truth was, the reason the girl was failing math class was she was on a totally different channel than her teacher. For instance, if a teacher is communicating through the visual channel and talks really fast and a student is kinesthetic and thinks slower, the student will struggle to keep up with the teacher's rapid-fire style of teaching. A visual teacher will often teach with visual aids, like drawing on a chalkboard and using a computer screen, while a kinesthetic student learns best through hands-on lessons, where they get to touch and hold. Sometimes issues in classes come down to the student not comprehending the teacher's style of communication. Visual students can struggle if an auditory teacher only lectures for an hour without using any visual aids to show examples of what's being taught. So, often when students are struggling, it could be due to having teachers who teach on different channels. One thing that will help is teaching your kids about the different channels and how to build rapport with their teachers.

I taught the girl who was struggling in math about rapport skills and how to speak in the teacher's channel. After that, this girl was forever changed. The next six weeks she went from failing to a B+, and six weeks after that she was making an A. It was incredible to see a young child understand this powerful distinction of story vs. meaning. Not only understand it, but she was able to have such a profound breakthrough that radically transformed her and improved her life. Simply changing the meaning of her story of what happened helped so much with boosting her self-esteem and confidence.

Another distinction that is very useful and really important when dealing with children is to remember that behavior isn't who we are. Behavior is what we do. I worked with a seven-year-old boy and his mother focused on this one distinction and it changed both their lives. The boy was playing baseball in the backyard with a friend. He didn't want to come inside for dinner because he was having so much fun playing outside. When the mother insisted that it was time to stop, he threw the ball at the house and it shattered a window by accident.

The mother freaked out and shouted at him, "You are such a bad boy."

He felt terrible and ashamed. He was punished for being "bad" and disobedient. When I worked with him, he actually thought that he was a bad person now. While his behavior was bad, it didn't mean that his whole being was bad. When I shared that with his mother, she had no idea that he felt that he was a bad person. Luckily we were able to teach the boy that behavior isn't who we are. It's what we do. We all have had "bad" behavior at some time in our lives.

— BEHAVIOR ISN'T WHO WE ARE. BEHAVIOR IS WHAT WE DO. —

Make sure that your children are not making it mean that they are bad people. If you've had behaviors that aren't the best and you're still making them mean something negative about yourself, then it's time to really understand this distinction. It doesn't justify a bad behavior in anyway. It does allow you to stop making it mean that you are a bad person for the rest of your life.

This one distinction of *separating the meaning from the story* can make all the difference in your life. It sure did mine. If there are any traumatic or negative events from the past that you have a story about, a good practice is to ask yourself, "What did I make that mean or What am I making it mean?" Then ask yourself, "Is this true or is this just a story I gave that meaning to? Is the interpretation positive or useful?" If it isn't then change the meaning of it. Especially if it's something negative you've been believing about yourself that isn't the truth. The freedom in letting go of the meaning to the stories can transform your life. This information can help heal your relationships, and most of all, heal yourself.

Communication Code 20

AVOID MISMATCHING

What is Mismatching?

Mismatching is the opposite of matching. When a person is a mismatcher, they will say the opposite to most things you say. Another name for a mismatcher is Exception Generator. They want to be the exception to the rule. Usually to be right. They will find a fault or flaw to what you're saying. They won't agree with you no matter what your talking about. When you match someone, you look for similarities in the situation or behavior that is in common to yourself. Matching is the basis of rapport. You tend to agree more and go along with people, and communication flows much better. When you mismatch, you make the other person wrong and say the total opposite of what they say. Or you come up with exceptions to everything they propose.

— MISMATCHING IS
A RAPPORT BREAKER. —

Mismatching breaks rapport, creates conflict, and disrupts the conversation. We have both of these behavioral options in us. We usually tend to lean to one style more than another in certain situations. Do you find that you're matching or mismatching people or your partner?

Mismatching has been the number one issue and constant complaint I hear from couples that causes the most fights, upsets, and frustration in their relationships. This chapter is to teach you how to become more aware if you are a mismatcher, how to stop mismatching and stop breaking rapport. The term *mismatcher* isn't used to judge, criticize, or label someone. It is a way to better understand how this form of communication pushes people away and creates unnecessary friction. Learning to stop mismatching will ultimately help you communicate better and more effectively with everyone. These tools and techniques will create a foundation in your relationship that will serve as a guide to help restore any conflicts, opposition, or discord.

Let me start by saying I used to mismatch people all the time. I broke rapport on a daily basis and didn't even know I was doing it. I said the opposite to be right constantly. I would argue and disagree on purpose, because I had no understanding about rapport, nor did I know that I was the biggest Exception Generator/Mismatcher ever. I just wanted to be right and be the exception to the rule. At that time, it was very difficult to be in conversation and relationships with me. I can't imagine where my life would be now if I hadn't learned about rapport and how to stop mismatching.

I will never forget when I was in a training and the leader called me out in front of the class and said, "You are the biggest mismatching exception generator I have ever met!"

"No, I'm not!" I shot back, still totally not getting it. Well, I must confess that it took a long while for me to not only get it but to learn how to stop being such a mismatcher. It takes practice and most of all an awareness that you are doing it. How do you know if you don't know? You don't. Become conscious and start noticing in yourself now if you are a mismatcher. Ask yourself if you're always trying to be right, if you argue with people often and make them wrong. If someone suggests something, do you quickly come back with an exception of why not to do what they suggest? Being aware of when you are mismatching will make it easier to recognize the behavior in someone else.

You could say that my karma came back when I took in my thirteen-year-old little sister to live with me in Dallas, Texas. I was much older than her, and I had no idea how much work it was going to be. Raising my little sister has been one of my greatest accomplishments.

She was one of the worst mismatchers I had ever seen, even worse than I was. Anything I would say, she would say the opposite. If I said, "It's raining," she would say, "No it's not. It's only sprinkling." If I would say, "Let's bring your lunch to school," she would say, "No, I want to buy my lunch." It was a constant struggle with her. I had worked with children for many years and had never seen a child so oppositional and defiant. This child mismatched so much that it was very difficult to be around her.

My sister was in 7th grade when she came to live with me. She had difficulty making friends because she mismatched everyone. She would make them wrong and say the opposite to just about anything they would say. It was such a battle with her and exhausting just being around her. I told her that when she was ready to learn how to stop mismatching and how to create rapport with people, and to start "watering" them with compliments and kindness, then I would be happy to teach her. By the end of that school year she finally asked for help. You couldn't believe how much this girl changed in one summer after I worked with her. She stopped mismatching and making people wrong. She learned how to create rapport, and by the end of that year, she had made so many friends who loved her. We were back in rapport and life with my sister became much easier and way more fun.

I have discovered this one key that will teach you how to stop mismatching, stop making people wrong, and how to stop breaking rapport. This simple 3-step process will help you learn how to communicate easier and more effectively. Or, if you're not a mismatcher, how to maintain rapport and connection when you're dealing with one. I will share some stories and give examples to make it easier to learn. It will take some practice and a lot of patience on your part. Once you've learned this one piece of information and put it into practice, it can transform your relationships, and most of all, your life.

Step by Step

1. Validate what people are saying.

This is the most important when dealing with a mismatcher, because their main purpose for mismatching is to be right. You can still have your own opinion or point of view if you validate someone first. For example, I never eat pecans. I have a bad reaction to them so I don't eat them. Well, when my sister was in 8th grade, we were getting along great. She came home from a friend's house and brought home two little pecan pies that her friend's mother had made for us. My sister ran into the house so excited and said to me, "You're going to love these pecan pies. They are so delicious!"

Now, she knew I didn't eat pecans; she had just forgotten. So the first thing I said to validate her feelings was, "Wow, you love pecan pie, don't you?" I didn't want to make her wrong in any way or mismatch her by telling her, "I don't eat pecan pies. You know that." I recognized she was being very thoughtful. I really didn't want to break rapport or mismatch her, so I made sure I validated her first. This avoided triggering her unconscious need to be right and mismatch me.

2. "I prefer..."

After I validated my sister, I said, "I prefer pumpkin pie." When you say "I prefer" instead of saying "I don't like this or that," it doesn't make the other person wrong, nor do you mismatch in any way that breaks rapport. Make sure you always validate what the person is saying first, even if you are not in agreement with them. When you validate first, then say what you "prefer" second, then you can maintain rapport with the person.

Another example: say you are on a date and you both are in the car together, listening to music. The Beatles are playing on the radio and your date says, "I just love the Beatles, don't you?" If you don't like them, you would never say, "No, I don't like the Beatles." Once you say the opposite you just made that person wrong, or at least they may feel as if you invalidated them, which breaks rapport. Instead, validate what your date just said, and say, "Oh, you love the Beatles, don't you? I prefer Aerosmith." By validating the person and saying "I prefer" then you will create even more rapport, while still being authentic about what you like.

3. Give compassion, empathy, and understanding.

After I told my sister that I "preferred" pumpkin pie, she began to beat herself up and say, "I'm so stupid. I totally forgot you don't eat pecans. What was I thinking?"

This third step is to use if anyone ever starts to berate themselves. What I said to her was "That was so thoughtful and kind of you to think of me! Guess what? Now there is more pie for you." She lit up and was so happy because she got to eat all of the pecan pies.

Giving empathy, compassion, and understanding will usually stop a mismatcher. Agreeing with them first, as much as possible, will also help. You want to do whatever you can to stop someone from beating themselves up. Remember, when you are not able to create rapport with people, then your communication will have little effect. Because I was able to water my sister with compliments and let her know that she was being thoughtful and kind, that made all the difference in the world. This is very important to do when speaking with children.

When dealing with an extreme mismatcher, try doing reverse psychology on them. Tell them to do the exact opposite of what you want them to do.

When making statements or a request, state them in the negative. Say things like:

"You're probably not going to want to do this."

"You probably won't like this.

"You probably won't understand."

If they are an extreme mismatcher, then they really don't want to be wrong and they especially don't want you to be right. So they will usually agree with you, because if not, then you will get to be right.

It's not just children and teenagers who mismatch.

Adults can be mismatchers too. I will never forget when I went to get a checkup and the doctor was such an extreme mismatcher. I had never encountered anyone who mismatched every question, statement, or comment that I said. It was annoying but I didn't take it personally, because she didn't have a clue. Most people don't know that they are mismatching, breaking rapport, and making communication difficult. It wasn't my place to tell this doctor anything to change her behavior and improve her rapport skills, although I really wanted to.

If you haven't recognized in yourself yet if you are a mismatcher, then ask the people around you if you say the opposite to most things they say or if you are argumentative. Are you more in agreement with them or do you tend to disagree more? Do you try to stir up a debate over every little thing? Are you the type who always has to be right? Most people mismatch from time to time even if they are aware. If you see that you mismatch others, it is a habit you're going to have to learn to break if you want to avoid arguments, frustration, friction, tension, and a feeling of disconnection in your communication, most importantly with your partner.

— FOCUSING ON WHAT YOU HAVE IN COMMON AND ESTABLISHING RAPPORT REDUCE CONFLICT AND CREATE HARMONY. —

I worked with a family who had three children, all teenagers. The entire family were mismatchers. They argued, fought, and disagreed about anything and everything. There was no rapport or communication with each other, and they didn't seem to like one another very much either. This family didn't know how to listen, nor did they want to listen. I wasn't sure if I was even going be able to help them, because they were so much into making each other wrong. Their situation was one of the worst cases I had ever witnessed in my entire career. They were very difficult people and didn't know how to communicate well at all.

I went to their home and met the whole family. It was shocking how disconnected they all were with one other. The first thing I had to do was create rapport with each of them. I asked questions to find out what they all were interested in and to get the kids to open up and start talking. My goal was to find out what each of them wanted for themselves and for the family. It was very clear that they had no idea what they wanted. They did know, however, what they *didn't* want, which was where we started with the session.

The first thing I shared with them was that they need-ed to learn how to listen and stop interrupting. I let them know that they all would have a chance to share how they're feeling and reassured them that I was there to help. I taught them about creating rapport with not only their family but with anyone they meet. The biggest breakthroughs came after I taught them about mismatching and how to stop doing it. Within two hours of spending time with this family the truth came out. These kids saw how much their parents argued and fought and they felt helpless. The kids wanted the arguing and fighting to stop. The parents recognized how much they mismatched each other, and finally they began to understand the impact that it was having on their children. The teenage kids were doing what they saw from their parents.

I worked with this family three times for two hours each session. You would not believe how much this family grew within this time. I also did private sessions with the parents and taught them about boundaries and better communication with their kids, and of course, with themselves. This information helped transform this family, and the kids were so happy that the parents were getting along better.

Start today by noticing in your family or in your relationship if you are mismatching. If one of you is mismatching, then it's time to work on learning the information in this chapter and applying the techniques. This way will help you break the habit and create a healthier connection with your family and with your partner. It will make all the difference in your life once you take responsibility and become more aware of how you are communicating.

Conclusion

Communication is like a puzzle. When you have the right pieces it fits together and creates a beautiful picture. It can be that simple when you have the correct communication codes, tools, skills, and information. Your ability to communicate with others clicks into place easier.

Imagine who you will be now once you practice building rapport with anyone, learning to interact in another person's channel, and noticing how your connection with people improves. Imagine who you will be when you are able to set boundaries, identify story vs. meaning, and learn to stop getting defensive and blaming others.

All of these communication codes work together to help you communicate more effectively with anyone. Every code brings new awareness about yourself and other people. From learning to release emotional baggage, to becoming a better listener, or being willing to face your shadow. You now have the pieces (codes). It's up to you see the bigger picture and utilize this new information. Practicing these codes daily will make you a great communicator. The quality of your relationships will improve and become deeper and more intimate.

If only I had known while growing up how to better understand communication and use many of these skills and tools, it would have made life a lot easier. Especially when it came to my relationships and connecting more with my family. Learning and applying all these communication skills has allowed me to create my dream. Living on Maui was a dream of mine for many years. I want you to know that dreams really do come true.

It has been such an honor to share my experiences and many things that I've learned with you. My hope and desire for you is that this book has brought more awareness, understanding, knowledge, and information to you in a way that you can radically improve your relationships and your life. That, from now on, you can communicate better with others, and most of all, with yourself. I hope that you will continue to allow yourself to learn, grow, and be open to new ways of communicating. That you are now more inspired to work on yourself and know that you can make more of a powerful impact in other people's lives.

As we say in Hawaii, aloha and mahalo.

Donza Doss is an NLP Master Trainer, Certified Master Hypnotherapist, life coach, author, speaker, and seminar leader based in Maui, Hawaii.

To book Donza on a radio show, TV show, public speaking event, or for coaching sessions, contact her at donzadoss@gmail.com.

CPSIA information can be obtained
at www.ICGtesting.com
Printed in the USA
BVHW030447130619
550812BV00001B/152/P